GORE VIDAL

——— ✳ ———

Point to Point
Navigation

——— ✳ ———

A MEMOIR
1964 TO *2006*

ABACUS

First published in the USA by Doubleday
First published in Great Britain in 2006 by Little, Brown
This paperback edition published in 2007 by Abacus

This book contains excerpts from *How to be an Intellectual in the Age of TV:
The Lessons of Gore Vidal* by Marcie Frank. Copyright © 2005 Duke University
Press. Reprinted with the kind permission of Duke University Press.

Photo credits appear on page 267.

Book design by Caroline Cunningham.

A CIP catalogue record for this book
is available from the British Library.

ISBN 978-0-349-12022-5

Papers used by Abacus are natural, recyclable products made from
wood grown in sustainable forests and certified in accordance with
the rules of the Forest Stewardship Council.

Printed and bound in Great Britain by Clays Ltd, St Ives plc
Paper supplied by Hellefoss AS, Norway

Abacus
An imprint of
Little, Brown Book Group
100 Victoria Embankment
London EC4Y 0DY

An Hachette Livre UK Company

www.littlebrown.co.uk

Gore Vidal ... ny screenplays,
more than ... oir *Palimpsest*.
Vidal's *Un... ... ...* won the National Book Award.

Praise for *Point to Point Navigation*

'Takes up ... his wonderful *Palimpsest* left off, recounting the Gore Vidal
journey from 1964 until 200?' William Boyd, *Mail on Sunday* Books of the Year

'Vidal has never been in excess ... ... observations are tossed off on page
after page with a c... ... ... finely observed
and always ... ... that there is
no dying of the lig...'

'It's a relief to read ... ... good ... wrong in
America from one of its most intelligent ... Vidal's world-view: he has a
fierce, uncontaminated sense of what's right and wrong, and he expresses his
most intimate opinions ... ... Simpson,
Daily Ma...

'Vidal's superior da... ... ... is utterly irresistible'
Christopher Hart, *...* of the Year

'A memoir ... ... out of the elevator, and *Point
to Point N...* ... ... positively his
last appea...

'We can't afford to lo... ... ... witty grandees ...
He's determined to ... ... not just surrender to the
average of ... ... *Palimpsest* was for
romance, ... Ultimately, this new
memoir is ... not pows... ... moving, what can be said. It is the mirror
image of a ... and ... ... *Scotsman*

'The weather in *Po... ...* ... ... has many sunny intervals, as we would
expect from this most polished and waspishly witty observer ... His description
of the moment of his beloved's death is a marvel of judgment and control ...
Montaigne himself could not have been more economical, more restrained or
more affecting' *Irish Times*

'These memoirs, with their psychological frankness and self-awareness and
their total engagement with our times, are quite as good as *Palimpsest* and that's
very good indeed' *Sunday Tribune*

ALSO BY GORE VIDAL

This final memoir is dedicated to Barbara Zimmerman Epstein, 1928–2006, who managed in her final days to keep an editorial eye on this text as she had done throughout the decades of our friendship on so many others: now whom shall I check this with to see if the tone is right? GV

AUTHOR'S NOTE

———— ✳ ————

"Point to Point Navigation": In World War Two I served as first mate of an army freight-supply ship based in the Aleutian Islands, where the weather was so bad that we seldom saw the sun much less moon and stars; this made it nearly impossible to use the compass to chart a course. Instead, we relied on maps where we had memorized various points or landmarks as guides, a process known as "point to point navigation," a process with obvious dangers (we had no radar). As I was writing this account of my life and times since *Palimpsest*, I felt as if I were again dealing with those capes and rocks in the Bering Sea that we had to navigate so often with a compass made inoperable by weather.

ONE

---- ✳ ----

The Influence of the Movies on My Generation: The Backstory

As I now move, graciously, I hope, toward the door marked Exit, it occurs to me that the only thing I ever really liked to do was go to the movies. Naturally, Sex and Art always took precedence over cinema but neither ever proved to be as dependable as the filtering of present light through that moving strip of celluloid which projects past images and voices onto a screen. Thus, in a seemingly simple process, screening history. (My book of that name has been allowed to go out of print and so I now reprise its principal argument.)

As writer and political activist, I have accumulated a number of cloudy trophies in my melancholy luggage. Some real, some imagined. Some acquired from life, such as it is; some from movies, such as they are. Sometimes, in time, where we are as well as were, it is not easy to tell the two apart. Do I wake or sleep?

I was born October 3, 1925, on the twenty-fifth birthday of Thomas Wolfe, the novelist not the journalist. I have lived through three-quarters of the twentieth century, and about one-third of the history of the United States of America. Briefly, what has been your impression thus far, Mr. Vidal? as eager interviewers are wont to ask. *Well*, it could have been worse, I begin with a calculated understatement. Then the Japanese recording machine goes on the blink and while the interviewer tries to fix it, he asks me to tell him, off the record, what was Marilyn Monroe really like? As I barely knew her, I tell him.

It is a universal phenomenon that whether one is at Harvard or at Oxford or at the University of Bologna, after the dutiful striking of attitudes on subjects of professional interest, like semiology, the ice does not break until someone mentions the movies. Suddenly, everyone is alert and adept. There is real passion as we speak of the falling-off of Fellini in recent years (of which more later) or of Madonna's curious contours and have they yet passed the once-disputed border of mere androgyny, arriving at some entirely new sexual continuum? Movies are the lingua franca of the twentieth century. The Tenth Muse, as they call the movies in Italy, has driven the other nine right off Parnassus— or off the peak, anyway.

Recently I observed to a passing tape recorder that I was once a famous novelist. When assured, politely, that I was still known and read, I explained myself. I was speaking, I said, not of me personally but of a category to which I once belonged that has now ceased to exist. I am still here but the category is not. To speak today of a famous novelist is like speaking of a famous cabinetmaker or speedboat designer. Adjective is inappropriate to noun. How can a novelist be famous—no matter how well known he may be personally to the press?—if the novel itself is of little consequence to the civilized, much less to the generality? The novel as teaching aid is something else, but hardly famous.

There is no such thing as a famous novelist now, any more than there is such a thing as a famous poet. I use the adjective in the strict sense. According to authority, to be famous is to be much talked about, usually in a favorable way. It is as bleak and inglorious as that. Yet thirty years ago, novels were actually read and discussed by those who did not write them or, indeed, even read them. A book *could* be famous then but today's public seldom mentions a book unless, like *The Da Vinci Code*, it is being metamorphosed into a faith-challenging film.

Contrary to what many believe, literary fame has nothing to do with excellence or true glory or even with a writer's position in the syllabus of a university's English Department, itself as remote to the Agora as Academe's shadowy walk. For any artist, fame is the extent to which the Agora finds interesting his latest work. If what he has written is known only to a few other practitioners, or to enthusiasts (Faulkner compared lovers of literature to dog breeders, few in number but passionate to the point of madness on the subject of bloodlines), then the artist is not only not famous, he is irrelevant to his time, the only time that he has; nor can he dream of eager readers in a later century as did Stendhal. If novels and poems fail to interest the Agora today, by the year 3091 such artifacts will not exist at all except as objects of monkish interest. This is neither a good nor a bad thing. It is simply not a famous thing.

Optimists, like the late John Gardner, regarded the university as a great good place where literature would continue to be not only worshipped but created. Perhaps he was right, though I do not like the look of those fierce theoreticians currently hacking away at the olive trees of Academe while seeding the Cephisus River with significant algae, their effect on the sacred waters rather like that of an oil spill off the coast of Alaska. Can there be a famous literary theoretician? Alas, no. The Agora has no interest in parlor games, other than contract bridge when one of the players is Omar Sharif. Literary theory is a glass-bead game whose reward for the ludic player is the knowledge that once he masters it, he will be thought by his peers to be ludicrous.

But I have lately been taken to task by an English teacher for my "intemperate" attacks on English Departments, which have, she noted ominously, cost me my place in the syllabus. So I shall now desist and, like Jonah, wait for that greatest of fishes to open wide his jaws and take me in. After all, if you miss one syllabus, there'll always be another in the next decade.

The best of our literary critics was V. S. Pritchett. I find fascinating his descriptions of what the world was like in his proletarian youth. Books were central to the Agora of 1914. Ordinary Londoners were steeped in literature, particularly Dickens. People saw themselves in literary terms, saw themselves as Dickensian types while Dickens himself, earlier, had mirrored the people in such a way that writer and Agora were, famously, joined; and each defined the other.

In London, Pritchett and I belonged to the same club. One afternoon we were sitting in the bar when a green-faced bishop stretched out his gaitered leg and tripped up a rosy-faced mandarin from Whitehall. As the knight fell against the wall, the bishop roared, "Pelagian heretic!" I stared with wonder. Pritchett looked very pleased. "Never forget," he said, "Dickens was a highly realistic novelist."

Today, where literature was movies are. Whether or not the Tenth Muse does her act on a theater screen or within the cathode tube, there can be no other reality for us since reality does not begin to *mean* until it has been made art of. For the Agora, Art is now sight and sound; and the books are shut. In fact, reading of any kind is on the decline. Half the American people never read a newspaper. Half never vote for president—the same half?

TWO

———————— ✳ ————————

In 1925, the year that I was born, *An American Tragedy*, *Arrowsmith*, *Manhattan Transfer*, and *The Great Gatsby* were published. A nice welcoming gift, I observed to the Three Wise Men from PEN who attended me in my cradle, a bureau drawer in Washington, D.C.'s Rock Creek Park. I shall be worthy! I proclaimed; shepherds quaked.

For a moment, back then, it did look as if Whitman's dream of that great audience which would in turn create great writers had come true. Today, of course, when it comes to literacy, the United States ranks number twenty-three in the world. I have no idea what our ranking was then, but though the popular culture was a predictable mix of jazz and the Charleston and Billy Sunday, we must have had, proportionately, more and better readers then than now; literature was a part of life, and characters from contemporary fiction, like Babbitt, entered the language, as they had done in Pritchett's youth and before. Our public educational system was also a good one. Certainly the *McGuffey's Eclectic*

*Reader*s of my grandfather's day would now be considered intolerably highbrow.

True, the Tenth Muse was already installed atop Parnassus, but she was mute. Actually, the movies were not as popular in the twenties as they had been before the First World War. Even so, in the year of my birth, Chaplin's *The Gold Rush* was released, while in my second year there appeared not only DeMille's *The Ten Commandments* as well as, no doubt in the interest of symmetry, *Flesh and the Devil* with Greta Garbo; it was also in my second year that the Tenth Muse suddenly spoke those minatory words "You ain't heard nothin' yet." Thus, the moving *and* talking picture began.

I saw and heard my first movie in 1929. My father and mother were still unhappily married and so we went, a nuclear family melting down, to the movies in St. Louis, where my father was general manager of TAT, the first transcontinental airline, later to merge with what became TWA.

I am told that as I marched down the aisle, an actress on the screen asked another character a question, and I answered her, in a very loud voice. So, as the movies began to talk, I began to answer questions posed by two-dimensional fictional characters thirty times my size.

My life has paralleled, when not intersected, the entire history of the talking picture. Although I was a compulsive reader from the age of six, I was so besotted by movies that one Saturday in Washington, D.C., where I grew up, I saw five movies in a day. It took time and effort and money to see five movies in a day; now, with television and videocassettes and DVDs, the screen has come to the viewer and we are all home communicants.

I don't think anyone has ever found startling the notion that it is not *what* things are that matters so much as *how* they are perceived. We perceive sex, say, not as it demonstrably is but as we think it ought to be as carefully distorted for us by the churches and the schools, and by— triumphantly—the movies, which are, finally, the only validation to which that dull anterior world, reality, must submit.

THREE

———————— ✳ ————————

The screening by CNN of our latest wars is carefully directed by those
who are producing the wars. What these serial wars are all about is still
not clear to us, nor are we ever apt to know what really happened until
someone makes a backstage movie like *The Bad and the Beautiful* or,
perhaps, *Platoon in the Desert*, a bitter, powerful film, quite as unrealis-
tic, in its way, as the CNN-Pentagon releases.

In February 1991 history was being invented before our eyes. From
day to day we saw the editing and dubbing process at work. But we
were merely viewers, while the actors on-screen were also, in an eerie
way, passive: part of a process no one seemed to be in control of.
Rumsfeld who now seeks to produce the sequels is, despite his elfin
charms, no more than a thousand points of pulsing light in a cathode
ray tube.

A few years ago while giving the Massey Lectures at Harvard the
mood of prophecy was upon me! "We shall yet be invited," I said, "by

the sponsors of USA, Inc., to bear witness to a presidential election in which one of the heroes of the Gulf will confront the politically ambitious Terminator." Yes, it will be someone like Rumsfeld versus Schwarzenegger, the ultimate screen version of my own old movie *The Best Man*, whose title was, of course, ironic.

FOUR

———————— ✳ ————————

I was struck by Eudora Welty's contribution to Harvard's Massey Lectures, published as *One Writer's Beginnings*. I have not her courage when it comes to speaking of my own life. I have also never been my own subject. But I do like the way that she set *her* scene, in Jackson, Mississippi, where her life and her life as a writer began. She starts, as everyone must, with a family. I could do the same, but do I dare? Contrary to legend, I was born of mortal woman, and if Zeus sired me, there is no record on file in the Cadet Hospital at the U.S. Military Academy, West Point. But if I was usually born, there my resemblance to other writers ends. My mother did not shop; and my father was not cold and aloof, nor was he addicted to the sports page of the newspapers. Unlike most American fathers—sons, too—he did not live vicariously. He was his own hero, and the Agora had loved him for a time. He had been an all-American football player at West Point, and he had represented the United States in the pentathlon at the Olympic Games. Later, he started three airlines. He was, I like to believe, the first person to realize that

there was absolutely no point to cellophane as opposed to blessed celluloid.

"DuPont just invented this," he said, presenting me with a glassy
cylinder. We unrolled the cellophane. "What's it for?" I asked. "Nothing!" He spoke with a true inventor's delight. For a season, in the thirties, one could see in the movie musicals cellophane used as curtains,
tablecloths, showgirl dresses. Finally, cellophane, unlike celluloid, ended
up as irrelevant wrapping. Yet it was nice in itself, like today's novel, say,
or, as Cole Porter apostrophized in "You're the Top," "You're cellophane!"

Did my kindly maternal grandfather—from Mississippi, just like
Eudora's—preside over a hardware business in Oklahoma City? No.
From two unrelated accidents, he was blind at the age of ten. He put
himself through law school, memorizing texts that were read to him by
a cousin. At thirty-seven, having helped invent the state of Oklahoma—
wit of this sort runs in our family—he became their famous senator.

Did my mother play bridge, bake pies in the kitchen, and perhaps
drink too much of the cooking sherry? On the contrary, she was a flap-
per very like her coeval, Tallulah Bankhead. (Faulkner went to his grave
believing that coeval meant evil at the same time as.) In appearance she
was a composite of Bette Davis and Joan Crawford. She never baked a
pie, but she did manage to drink, in the course of a lifetime, the equivalent of the Chesapeake Bay in vodka. Eudora's people, just south of
where the Gores lived, thought my mother fast. They were right. She
married and divorced not only my famous father but a rich stockbroker; then she married a famous air force general, who promptly died.
Meanwhile, the stockbroker married a woman whose daughter married
a man who was elected president only to have his head shot in as the
two of them were driving through Dallas on a hot November day. What
is one to do, fictionally, with a family that has itself become a pervasive
fiction that continues to divert the Agora? Later, I will try to reveal what
actually happened that terrible day in Dallas.

I tried, once, to deal with my early days in a novel with no particular key but a number of what I still think to be cunning locks. It was called *Washington, D.C.* I centered my narrative on the two houses where I grew up: that of Senator Gore in Rock Creek Park—now, significantly, the Malaysian embassy—and that of my stepfather, the ill-named Merrywood, high above the Potomac River on the road to Manassas. Each house represented a different world that I would either have to master or be mastered by, the common fate of most children of Agora-noted families. All in all, I fancied this book. I was there and not there in the text. I had revealed and not revealed my peculiar family. I had also, without intending to, started on a history of the American Republic as experienced by one family and its emblematic connection to Aaron Burr.

During the next quarter century I re-dreamed the Republic's history, which I have always regarded as a family affair. But what was I to do with characters that were—are—not only famous but even preposterous? When my mother was asked why, after three famous marriages, she did not try for a fourth, she observed, "My first husband had three balls. My second, two. My third, one. Even *I* know enough not to press my luck."

At the time, *Washington, D.C.* was regarded as a novelized MGM movie, with sets by Cedric Gibbons and a part for Katharine Hepburn at her most mannered. So much for my strict realism. Eudora Welty may tell us all about *her* folks, and there is the pleasurable shock of recognition. But should I capture my family upon the page, the result is like a bad movie—or, worse, a good one. I never again used my immediate family as the stuff of fiction. We require no less than a Saint Simon. Unfortunately, we have received no more than a Kitty Kelley. What is the Agora trying to tell us?

It is possible that even when working from memory, I saw the world in movie terms, as who did not or, indeed, who does not? So let us examine the way in which one's perceptions of history were—and are—dominated by illustrated fictions of great power, particularly those screened in childhood.

Although most of the movie palaces of my Washington youth no longer exist, I can still see and smell them in memory. There was Keith's, across from the Treasury, a former vaudeville house where Woodrow Wilson used to go. Architecturally, Keith's was a bit too classically spacious for my taste. Also, the movies shown tended to be more stately than the ones to be seen around the corner in Fourteenth Street. Of course, no movie was ever truly dull, even the foreign ones shown at the Belasco in Lafayette Park, located, I believe, in the house of a fictional character of mine, known to history as William Seward, the purchaser of Alaska.

It was at the Belasco that I first saw myself screened in a Pathé newsreel. At the age of ten I took off and landed a plane. As Roosevelt's director of air commerce, my father was eager to popularize a cheap, private plane that was, if not foolproof, childproof. Yet, thinking back, though he had grasped the silliness of cellophane, he seriously believed that since almost everyone could now afford a car, so almost everyone should be able to afford a plane. He dedicated years of his life to putting a cheap plane in every garage. Thanks to his dream, I, too, was famous for a summer. In a recent biography, I noted with amusement that one of the numerous lies that Truman Capote had told his childhood friend Harper Lee was that at the age of ten *he* had flown a plane.

Today anyone's life can be filmed from birth to death thanks to the video camera. But for my generation there was no such immortality unless one were a movie star or a personage in the newsreels. Briefly, I was a newsreel personage. But what I really wanted to be was a movie star: specifically, I wanted to be Mickey Rooney, and to play Puck, as he had done in *A Midsummer Night's Dream*.

Parenthetically, life is always more ironic than art. While I was acting several lectures at Harvard (and revealing for the first time my envy of Mickey Rooney), Rooney was at the bookstore of the Harvard Coop, autographing copies of his latest *book*.

Recently I watched my famous flight for the first time since 1936. I am now old enough to be my father's father. He looks like the movie star. I don't. I am small, blond, with a retroussé nose as yet unfurled in all its Roman glory. I am to fly the plane, and a newsreel crew is on hand to record the event. My father was a master salesman: "This is your big chance to be a movie star," he had said. "All you have to do is remember to take off into the wind." As I had flown the plane before, I am un-afraid. I swagger down the runway, crawl into the plane, and pretend to listen to my father's instructions. But my eyes are not on him but on the cobra-camera's magic lens. Then I take the plane off; fly it; land with a bump; open the door; and face my interviewer.

"What fools these mortals be," Mickey's speech, as Puck, is sound-ing in my ears as I start to speak but cannot speak. I stare dumbly at the camera. My father fills in; then he cues me. What was it like, flying the plane? I remember the answer that he wants me to make: "It was as easy as riding a bicycle." But I had argued, doggedly, that it was a lot more complicated than riding a bicycle. Anyway, I am trapped in the wrong script. I say the line. Then I make a face to show my disapproval and, for an instant, I resemble not Mickey Rooney but Peter Lorre in *M*. My screen test had failed.

In 1935 I had seen Max Reinhardt's film, *A Midsummer Night's Dream*. Bewitched, I read the play, guessing at half the words; then, ad-dicted to this strange new language, I managed to read most of Shake-speare before I was sixteen. (Yes, *Cymbeline*, too.) I am sure that my response was not unique. Certainly, other children must have gone to Shakespeare's text if only in search of Mickey and that Athenian forest where, after sunset, Oberon and Titania ride, attended by all sorts of mythical creatures; and those mortals who stray amongst them and, hence, are subject to change. Metamorphosis, not entropy, is sovereign in these woods, and to this day I can still, in reverie, transport myself to A Wood Near Athens on that midsummer night before the Athenian Duke's marriage to the Amazon Queen.

Washington's principal movie palaces were on the east side of Four-teenth Street. The Capitol was the grandest, with a stage show and an orchestra leader called Sam Jack Kaufman, whom I once saw in the drugstore next to the theater. He wore an orange polo coat that matched his orange hair. He bought a cigar. Between each movie showing, there was an elaborate stage show. I also remember Peter Lorre's hair-raising and ear-deafening impersonation of himself in *M*. Then, there were the Living Statues. Well-known historic tableaux were enacted by actors and actresses in white leotards. Sex could often be determined only by wig. Even so, the effect was awesome in its marblelike stillness. Boys in puberty, or older, affected lust when they saw these figures, but those of us who were prepubescent sternly looked only to the beauty and verisimilitude of the compositions. Thus, in many a youthful bosom, a Ruskin—or even a Rose LaTouche—was awakened.

The Metropolitan was my favorite of the small theaters. I think it was here that Warner Brothers pictures played. The atmosphere was raffish. And the gum beneath the seats was always fresh Dentyne. The Palace Theater was also congenial, while the Translux, devoted to news-reels and documentaries, was the only movie house to open in my time, and its supermodern art deco interior smelled, for some reason, of honey. At the time of the coronation of George VI, there was displayed in the lobby a miniature royal coach and horses. I wanted that coach more than I have ever wanted anything. But my father made an insuffi-cient offer to the manager of the theater. Later, I acquired the coach through my stepfather, to add to a collection of three thousand soldiers kept in the attic at Merrywood. Here I enacted an endless series of dra-mas, all composed by me. If ever there was a trigger to the imagination, it was those lead soldiers. Today they would be proscribed because war is bad and women under-represented in their ranks. But I deployed my troops for other purposes than dull battle. I was my own Walter Scott. I was the Warner Brothers, too, and Paramount as I played auteur, so like God, we have been told by film critics.

The most curious of the movie houses of my childhood was the Blue Hen at Rehoboth Beach, Delaware, where the family went occa-sionally in the summer. What a Blue Hen had to do with a movie house

I puzzled over for half a century until a young Delawarean in Harvard's Sanders Theatre told me that the Blue Hen was the state university mascot.

At the Blue Hen I saw *Love Song of the Nile* with Ramon Navarro and Helen Broderick: a film that I can find no record of anywhere except in my memory. But I do know that Egypt was on my mind as early as 1932 when I saw *The Mummy*, with Boris Karloff. The effect of that film proved to be lifelong. Also, it must be recalled that in those days if you saw a movie once, that was that. The odds were slim that you would ever see it again. There were no Museums of Modern Art or film retrospectives. Today, thanks to videocassettes and DVDs, one can see a film as often as one likes. But since we knew back then that we would have only the one encounter, we learned how to concentrate totally.

In a sense, learning a film at a single screening must have been something like a return to that oral tradition where one acquired a Homeric song through aural memory. In any case, at seven I confronted not the rage of Achilles but the obsession of a man three thousand years dead. I was never to forget my first sight of the mummy in its case as, nearby, an archaeologist reads a spell from an ancient papyrus. Slowly, the linen-wrapped hand moves. The archaeologist turns; sees what we cannot see; starts to laugh, and cannot stop laughing. He has gone mad.

Fifty-eight years later, I watched the movie for the first time since its release and I became, suddenly, seven years old again, mouth ajar, as I inhabited, simultaneously, both ancient Egypt and pre-imperial Washington, D.C. Then, as the film ended, my seven-year-old world dissolved, to be glimpsed no more except for the odd background shot of a city street, say, in a 1932 movie, where now-dead people are very much alive, unconscious of the screening camera as they go about their business, in the margins of a film where they are forever, briefly, alive.

What appeals in *The Mummy*, other than the charnel horror? Obviously, any confirmation that life continues after death has an appeal to almost everyone except enlightened Buddhists. No one wants to be extinct. Hence, the perennial popularity of ghost stories or movies about visits to heaven that prove to be premature since heaven can always wait even if hell be here.

For a time, after *The Mummy*, I wanted to become an archaeologist, though not like the one played by Bramwell Fletcher, whose maniacal laughter still haunts me. (Years later, Fletcher acted in the first play that I wrote for live television.) I preferred the other archaeologist in the film, as performed by David Manners, who also appeared in *Roman Scandals* (1933), another film that opened for me that door to the past where I have spent so much of my lifelong present.

From earliest days, the movies have been screening history, and if one saw enough movies, one learned quite a lot of simpleminded history. Steven Runciman and I met on an equal basis not because of my book *Julian*, which he had written about, but because I knew *his* field, thanks to a profound study not of his histories but of Cecil B. DeMille's *The Crusades* (1935), in which Berengaria, as played by Loretta Young, turns to her Lionheart husband and pleads, "Richard, you *gotta* save Christianity." A sentiment that I applauded at the time but came later to rethink.

Thanks to *A Tale of Two Cities*, *The Scarlet Pimpernel*, and *Marie Antoinette*, my generation of prepubescents understood at the deepest level the roots—the flowers, too—of the French Revolution. Unlike Dickens's readers, we *knew* what the principals looked and sounded like. We had been there with them.

In retrospect, it is curious how much history *was* screened in those days. Today, Europe still does stately tributes to the Renaissance, usually for television; otherwise, today's films are stories of him and her and now, not to mention daydreams of unlimited shopping with credit cards. Fortunately, with time even the most contemporary movie undergoes metamorphosis, *becomes* history as we get to see real life as it was when the film was made, true history glimpsed through the window of a then-new, now-vintage car.

My first and most vivid moviegoing phase was from 1932 to 1939—

from seven to fourteen. Films watched before puberty are still the most vivid. *A Midsummer Night's Dream, The Mummy, Roman Scandals, The Last Days of Pompeii.* Ancient Egypt, classical Rome, Shakespeare when he was still in thrall to that most magical of poets, Ovid.

Although *Roman Scandals* was a comedy, starring the vaudevillian Eddie Cantor, I was told not to see it. I now realize why the movie, which I saw anyway, had been proscribed. The year of release was 1933. The country was in an economic depression. Drought was turning to dust the heart of the country's farmland, and at the heart of the heart of the dust bowl was my grandfather's state of Oklahoma. So bad was the drought that many of his constituents were abandoning their farms and moving west to California. The fact that so many Oklahomans, Okies for short, were obliged to leave home was a very sore point with their senator.

At the beginning of *Roman Scandals* we see the jobless in Oklahoma. One of them is Eddie Cantor, who is knocked on the head and transported to ancient Rome, much as Dorothy was taken by whirlwind from Kansas to Oz; thus, a grim Oklahoma is metamorphosed into a comic-strip Rome.

FIVE

———————— ✳ ————————

My memory of the Depression is more of talk on the radio and in the house than of actual scenes of apple-selling in the street. Also, I did not always understand what I heard. When stock market shares fell, I thought that chairs were falling out of second-story windows. I did know that senators spent their days in the Senate chamber passing bills—dollar bills, I thought—from one to another, by no means an entirely surreal image.

At the age of five I sat in the Senate gallery and watched as T. P. Gore was sworn in for a fourth term. Defeated in 1920, he had made a triumphant return in 1930. I recall the skylit pale greens of the chamber so like the aquarium in the basement of the Commerce Building. I was also very much aware of my grandfather's enemy (and my father's friend and employer), the loudly menacing Franklin D. Roosevelt, with a black spot—like a dog's—over his left eyebrow. He was always in the papers and on the radio; worse, there he was in practically every newsreel, smiling balefully at us and tossing his huge head about.

Finally, in the spring of 1932, I saw at first hand history *before* it was screened. A thousand veterans of the First World War had arrived in the capital to demand a bonus for their services in the late and, to my grandfather, unnecessary war. These veterans were known as the Bonus Army, or Boners for short. By June, there were seventeen thousand of them encamped around Washington and in deserted buildings near the Capitol. The city panicked. There was talk of a revolution, like the recent one in Russia, or the one in France, which I knew so well from having seen so many movies.

At first, I thought that the Boners were just that—white skeletons like those jointed cardboard ones displayed at Halloween. Bony figures filled my nightmares until it was explained to me that these Boners were not from slaughterhouses but from poorhouses. My grandfather was against granting them a bonus. A onetime fiery populist from the Mississippi up-country, and a contributor to the only socialist constitution of the fifty states, he had come to the conclusion that "if there was any race other than the human race, I'd go join it." He was a genuine populist; but he did not like people very much. He always said no to anyone who wanted government aid. On one memorable occasion, the blind senator was denounced to his face by a blind suppliant for federal aid. On the other hand, he believed in justice—due process, anyway—for all, equally.

As the summer grew hotter and the Depression deepened, and Congress debated whether or not to give the veterans a bonus, rumors spread: *they* had attacked the White House; *they* had fired on the Capitol; and, most horribly, *they* were looting the Piggly Wiggly grocery stores. I dreamed of skeletons on the march; of Boris Karloff, too—all bones and linen wrapping.

On June 17, 1932, the Senate met to vote on the Bonus Bill. I drove with my grandfather to the Capitol, sitting beside him. Davis, his black driver and general factotum, was at the wheel. I stared out the open window, looking for Boners. Instead, I saw only shabby-looking men holding up signs and shouting at occasional cars. At the Senate side of the Capitol there was a line of policemen. Before we could pass through the line, Senator Gore was recognized. There were shouts; then a stone came through the open window of the car and landed with a crash on the floor between us. My grandfather's memorable words were: "Shut the window," which I did.

Shortly after, the Boners were dispersed by the army, headed by General MacArthur and his aide Major Eisenhower. Guns were fired; there were deaths. The following Sunday, my father and I flew low over what had been the Boners' encampment at the Anacostia Flats. There were still smoking fires where the shanties had been. The place looked like a garbage dump, which in a sense it had been, a human one.

From that moment on, I was alert to all films about the French and Russian revolutions and, from that day, I have always known that not only could *it* happen here but it probably would. In the wake of the disorders and discontents of the sixties, soon to rise again in the nineties, this is no great insight. But back then, it was an ominous portent of things to come, and of the fragility of our uniquely founded state in which everyone thought himself guaranteed sufficient liberty in order to pursue happiness on the high Jeffersonian ground that the present belongs to the living. But if the rich are too rich and the poor have nothing to support them in bad times, then *how* is liberty's tree to be nourished?

A chill wind went through the Republic. Three years later Social Security was passed by Congress despite the cry of the conservatives that this was godless socialism and henceforth every citizen would be forced to exchange his name for an administrative number. My grandfather asked for the bill to be voted on. His friend, Huey Long, seconded the motion. Then Senator Long voted for Social Security, and Senator Gore abstained.

The children of the famous are somewhat different from the children of all the rest, including those of the merely rich. Until my mother married a second time, there was no fortune in the family. Cunningly, my father managed to lose control of each of the airlines that he had founded; but then he had no interest in money, only in the making of new things. Senator Gore lived on his salary as a senator, $15,000 a year. He was also the first and, I believe, last senator from an oil state to die without a fortune. But though we were relatively poor, I could tell that I was not like the other children because of the questions that my teachers would ask me about my father and grandfather, and was it true what the papers said?

When I asked my grandparents about the newspapers, they replied in unison, "If you read it in the papers, it isn't true." But then populists have never had a good press in Freedom's Land. I was also warned never to answer the questions of strangers, and, of course, I always did. To one reporter, I said that my stepfather could not possibly have been the father of my half sister as he had not known my mother long enough. Although I had no inkling of the facts of life, I had an instinct for the telling detail. Later, at school, when asked what my father did, I said, "He's in the newspapers." Which seemed to me a precise way of accounting for his activities as director of air commerce.

In 1936 I moved from Rock Creek Park to the house, Merrywood, across the Potomac, and money suddenly hedged us all round. At the height of the Depression there were five servants in the house, *white servants*, a sign of wealth unique for Washington in those years. My stepfather was an heir to Standard Oil, the nemesis of T. P. Gore and Huey Long. Although I now lived the life of a very rich prince, I was still *unconscious* of class differences other than the relation between black and white, which was something as fixed in our city then as the Capitol dome, and as unremarkable. But the rock that had landed between my grandfather and me in the back of the car was a sharp and unmistakable signal that there were others who were not, indeed, princes at all; that there were millions of people to whom an old-fashioned word applied—pauper.

Although something of an avatar of Mark Twain, I have never read *The Prince and the Pauper*, made into a film by Warner Brothers in the thirties.

Lonely children often have imaginary playmates but I was never lonely; rather, I was solitary, and wanted no company at all other than books and movies, and my own imagination. I was Puck; I was a long-dead Egyptian; I was a time traveler to Rome; I was many other selves. But now, suddenly, I wanted to be not Puck, or even Mickey Rooney. I wanted to be the identical twin boys who played the prince and the pauper. I wanted to be myself, twice. I do not dare speculate upon what the school of Vienna—I refer, of course, to the Riding School—would make of this. But I don't think that my response to the film was unusual, particularly if one were the actors' age and so could easily identify with the notion of the two as really one and that one oneself, or with the general proposition that a palpable duplicate of oneself would be the ideal companion.

A current pejorative adjective is narcissistic. Generally, a narcissist is anyone better looking than you are, but lately the adjective is often applied to those "liberals" who prefer to improve the lives of others rather than exploit them. Apparently, a concern for others is self-love at its least attractive, while greed is now a sign of the highest altruism. But then to reverse, periodically, the meanings of words is a very small price to pay for our vast freedom not only to conform but to consume.

The childhood desire to be a twin does not seem to me to be narcissistic in the vulgar Freudian sense. After all, one is oneself; and the other other. It is the sort of likeness that makes for wholeness, and is it not that search for likeness, that desire and pursuit of the whole—as Plato has Aristophanes remark—that is the basis of all love? As no one has ever actually found wholeness in another human being, no matter of what sex, the twin is the closest that one can ever come toward wholeness with another; and, dare one invoke biology and the origin of our species, there is always, back of us mammals, doomed to die once we have procreated, our sexless ancestor the amoeba, which never dies as it does not reproduce sexually but merely—serenely?—breaks in two and identically replicates.

Anyway, I thought Billy and Bobby Mauch were cute as a pair of bug's ears, and I wished I were either one of them, *one* of them, mind you. I certainly did not want to be two of *me*, as one seemed more than

The Mauch twins as the Pauper and the Prince face to face. When the Prince read what I wrote about this mythic film he sent me an amiable letter and thus I entered, I felt, a magical narrative.

enough to go around even in a "famous" family. Yet doubleness has always fascinated me, as mirrors do, as filmed images do.

The plot is pure Shakespeare. It is also impure Samuel Clemens— or is he by now entirely Mark Twain? Certainly, he was obsessed by twins, and by the likeness of one to the other. But then what does his pen name mean? if it does not mean two or twain or twin? I often wonder what I might have become if Warner Brothers had filmed not *The Prince and the Pauper* but that blackest of American "twin" fables, *Pudd'nhead Wilson*.

Although Errol Flynn is charming as an ideal older brother, I had completely forgotten that he was in the movie. Plainly, I didn't want an older brother. I was fixated on the twins themselves. On the changing of clothes, and the reversal of roles. On the descent of the boy prince into the life of the poor, which struck many bells for someone who had actually seen the Boners plain. We now know, through such FBI informers as Ronald Reagan, that in the thirties and the forties Hollywood was being infiltrated by the Reds and that writers in the pay of Moscow were subtly poisoning every script that they could with malicious attacks on greed and selfishness and those other traits that have made our country great. It is true, of course, that some of the movie writers *were* Communists but, as they all agreed in later years, you couldn't get *anything* of a political nature into any film. This has also been true in my experience.

On the other hand, it is worth at least a doctoral thesis for some scholar to count how often in films of the thirties and forties a portrait of Franklin Roosevelt can be found, usually hanging on a post-office wall; and then try to discover who put it there: the writer, the director, the producer—the set designer?

At a subconscious level, there was actually a good deal of politics in even the simplest of everyday stories, while historical pieces could always conceal messages, since studios were certain that nothing that happened *then* could ever have anything at all to do with *now*. For me, at twelve, the poor of London in their encampment, Robbers' Roost, were just like the Boners in the Anacostia Flats.

The film's overt political message is straightforward: a good king will listen to the people and help them. Oddly enough, kings with absolute power were a staple of American movies. One seldom saw democracy in action and, when one did, the results were apt to be simpleminded fables like those of Frank Capra.

More is to be learned, I believe, from William Keighley, auteur of *The Prince and the Pauper* as well as of *Babbitt*, than from Capra. The prince's father, Henry VIII, explains to his son the nature of power. Why the Warner Brothers thought that the American public would find interesting a disquisition on princely power in Renaissance times is a secret that Jack L. Warner took to his grave. On the other hand, the king's musings were possibly addressed to the serfs at Warner Brothers, a studio known for its love of such traditions as the annual Christmas layoff.

The king confides: "Never trust too much, love too much, need anyone too much that you cannot betray them with a smile." This is true Machiavelli and must have seemed startling to an audience imbued with such Christian values as turning the other cheek while meekly obeying your master. But I am now convinced that my generation of Americans either went to church *or* to the movies for spiritual guidance. As a third-generation atheist, I was nourished by the screen, and I was particularly struck by the king's sermon, so like my grandfather's bleak wisdom. "In politics you must always treat an enemy as if he might one day be a friend, and a friend as if he might one day be an enemy." My grandfather did concede that he found the second part hard to do, but that did not make it any the less advisable.

The scene that I remembered best was a forest at night, much like A Wood Near Athens. The prince has been taken captive. He is told that he is to be killed right then and there with a knife. The lighting is beautiful, and if television ever decides to paint this black-and-white film, I hope they will use Gainsborough's delicate earth colors.

There is a startling close-up of the prince's face as he realizes that he is about to die. Then, invited to pray, he gets off a bold line: he hopes that his father is *not* watching from Heaven because the king would be

ashamed of the treacherous Englishman, but not of his son. I still feel
the force of this scene. For the first time, the boy knows that he is about
to stop being. Like most children, I often used to imagine what death
must be like. But unlike most, I had no belief, or even interest, in an afterlife. To me, if not the prince, death is *not* being; and that is why for
us who know only being, death is literally unimaginable, try as hard as
one might to imagine—what? An empty room where one is not? Put
out the light and then put out the light? For the young, death is
supremely unnatural. For the old, it is so natural that it is not worth
thinking about.

As I had never for an instant believed in an afterlife, I suppose that
all I could come up with, at twelve, was the formulation that as one was
not before birth, one will not be after death, and so there you are, or not,
as the case may be. For some, the notion of images impressed on celluloid provides a spurious sense of immortality, as does, indeed, the notion that those light rays which record our images will keep on bending
about the universe forever. There are those who find comfort in such
concepts. I don't.

Errol Flynn saves the prince in the wood, and as the pauper is about
to be crowned king, the true prince is restored, and all is right with a
world where a good boy-king will stand up to evil, whether played by
Claude Rains or by Hitler.

So, in a single film, screened at the susceptible time of puberty, one
experienced the shock, as it were, of twinship. Also, the knowledge of
how to exercise power. Also, the contrast between rich and poor that
even I had been made aware of as the Depression deepened, and there
was no help on earth for the poor except from the king, if he be good
and well-informed. This was much the attitude of the American people
at that time to their sovereigns, Franklin and Eleanor, who were opposed, as was the good prince, by evil lords. Finally, there is the impact
of imminent death upon a twelve-year-old. Of all the facts of life, death
is the oddest. Suddenly, there it is, in a moonlit forest, at the hand of a
traitor with a knife; and then no more life. No anything. Nothing.

Underlying the film, there is an appeal to altruism. Now altruism is a brief phase through which some adolescents must pass. It is rather like acne. Happily, as with acne, only a few are permanently scarred. Yet the prince in the film is obliged to note that there are others in the world beside himself (not to mention a pauper duplicate), and to those others he must be responsible. This is a highly un-American point of view but not without its charm for the youthful viewer, who will discover for himself, more soon than late, that one must always put oneself first, except when the American empire requires a war and then, *Dulce et decorum est pro patria mori*. I believe that my generation of Americans was the very last even to begin to take seriously that once-powerful invocation.

But now the feature film's over. The newsreel begins. The Japanese sink an American gunboat on a river in China. Senator Gore is defeated for a fifth term. "All is lost," he declares, "including honor." The House Un-American Activities Committee is formed. The director of air commerce resigns. The Munich Agreement is signed. Hitler takes over Czechoslovakia's Sudetenland.

I used to chat with Prince Philip of Hesse, the only person I ever knew who knew Hitler. Philip was son-in-law to King Victor Emmanuel of Italy, and Italy was a founding member—with Germany—of the Axis powers. Prince Philip was always regarded with suspicion by Hitler, and, eventually, his wife, Princess Mafalda, was sent off to a German concentration camp where she died during an air raid—Puccini had dedicated *Turandot* to her. Prince Philip was rarely revelatory. Like his class, he regarded Hitler as a cheap demagogue, who was bringing a degree of order to the country. I asked about anti-Semitism. Prince Philip said he thought at first it was just pandering to voters. "Later, of course, when friends of mine were proscribed, I tried to intervene. Hitler was always agreeable. He even protected them for a time. But I never got him past his usual point: 'in the professions they should never number more than their proportion in the general population,' which made no sense to me."

SIX

———————— ✳ ————————

Next: Previews of Coming Attractions. And coming to this theater is—what else?—*Fire Over England*, yet again. Huey Long is murdered.

My whole family delighted in Huey Long not for his politics but for his comic speechifying. After my father divorced my mother he rented an apartment in the same Connecticut Avenue building where Huey was bacheloring it. Though my father disliked most politicians, Huey always made him laugh. The Kingfish, as Long was known, began performing when he stepped out of the elevator in the morning and confronted the day in the form of a desk clerk, a meek young man, whom Huey enjoyed lecturing on Success, to the young man's embarrassment. Huey would declaim: "Why, when I was your age I would spend what little idle time I had with an instructive book not that racing form I see that you're now trying to hide. Of course I was not given to late-night dissipation in the fleshpots of the District of Columbia! Oh, you can't hide your ruinous habits from me! I can see by the trembling of your hands what demon rum is doing to you . . ." The poor clerk was indeed trembling—with terror—as the great voice thundered in his ears and Huey, particularly if an audience had now filled the lobby, would become prayerful as he invoked the lad's aged mother back in Butte, Montana. "I know how each night she prays for your success—on her knees, little suspecting that all those hours that should be golden with study are scarlet with vice . . ." Tears would fill Huey's eyes on cue as he contemplated that little old lady who had mothered a son so reprobate. Only my father's arrival with his car would stop the great flow of language, and Huey would cadge a ride from the director of air commerce while lecturing my father on aviation as they proceeded to the Capitol where Huey had all sorts of somber public advice for President Roosevelt.

Lately, Huey had been discussing a run for the presidency on a third-party ticket in 1936. Many thought he could keep FDR from being reelected and then in 1940 he would be the Democratic candidate and win the presidency. Possible? We shall never know. Huey was gunned down in the Louisiana State Capitol at Baton Rouge by a medical doctor with no known motive. It was rumored that Huey had actually been killed by his own guards. Forever after, the Long family believed that FDR had ordered his killing, which seems farfetched even in Louisiana. But it was about then that the *conspiracy theorist doctrine* was promulgated to make it impossible for anyone to investigate much of anything and so it was that we, a naturally suspicious and garrulous people, were officially silenced through our institutions and by a media seemingly devoted to a Sicilianesque omertà, even when Marine Corps General Smedley Butler revealed that he had been approached by right wing elements to overthrow FDR in his first term, a story that never really broke despite Butler's own memoir of the events. Huey's murder was the first of a number of stylized "unsolvable" murders committed by solitary lone killers given to motiveless acts of violence; witness, Lee Harvey Oswald at Dallas. More later. It is as if we have a permanent

The great Huey Long is ready to crown every man a king, until a mysterious doctor gunned him down in the Louisiana State Capitol. He was preparing to run for president on a third-party ticket, splitting FDR's vote for reelection.

Federal Bureau of Non-Investigation ever ready to chuckle about the relation between flying saucers and political assassinations or the "alleged" torture of those held in our military prisons.

In any event, Huey, whose slogan was "every man a king," never did have his proper day. But there is a wonderfully comic bit of newsreel where he is sampling a New Orleans bartender's Sazerac, a lethal cocktail full of whipped egg white. He praises his old friend behind the bar, sips delicately at the brew, and gives gentle instruction on the correct proportion of the ingredients. He finishes one glass which is refilled. Ever the perfectionist, he savors this ambrosia, complimenting the bartender—so let us leave the Kingfish there, contented, presidential, the people's friend who built so many schools, roads, hospitals, and gleefully taxed "The Standard Oil" to pay for it all.

SEVEN

─────────── ✳ ───────────

I sit now at a so-called partners desk where two people can sit directly across from each other. In 2003 my "partner" (as the politically correct call it) of fifty-three years—Howard Auster—died and now I work here alone. Here? Where? When? Who? We shall let "why" linger a while longer in the wings.

"Here" is the Hollywood Hills. "When" is today, December 31, 2004. New Year's Eve is at hand and with luck—good or bad—tomorrow will bring the two thousand fourth year of the Christian era to a close. For several days television has been full of images of Southeast Asia drowning in tsunami tidal waves. As I watched the Thai island of Phuket being pummeled by wind, I looked in vain for the Royal Yacht Club (a hotel not a club) where we stayed a dozen years ago. It is now as gone as, indeed, are "we" reduced to the singular "me." Rain has been falling for more than a week on Los Angeles. Since 1977 "we" have had a house here, usually rented out to others as neither of us ever had any intention of living here until the obligatory arrival of the Cedars-Sinai Hospital

Howard and I in Arizona during the filming of *Billy the Kid* with Val Kilmer. I play a minister whose specialty is—what else?—funerals. Over the years I've done several Billy the Kids, the first for live TV with Paul Newman in 1955. Others turned my work into the film *The Left Handed Gun*, a perfect mess almost as highly rated by the French as Jerry Lewis.

years which, finally, came two years ago, like a tsunami wind, for him. So now—"what?"

Barbara Epstein, editor of *The New York Review of Books*, has just rung to report a "what": the death of Susan Sontag whose decades-long war with cancer is over. Years ago a celebrated guru of the day gravely admonished her: "What's all the fuss about? Why don't you just let go? After all, death is simply a natural part of life," and so on. Susan was having none of this: "I don't consider death at my age," she said (she was still young—forties?), "to be just nothing," echoing Tennessee Williams who once wrote: "I have never considered death to be much in the way of completion." I last saw Susan when we acted in Norman Mailer's production of Shaw's *Don Juan in Hell*. I was the Devil; she was Donna Anna . . . What gifts Susan had for performance were reserved for her most successful portrayal—the autodidact who could play aspects of herself by ear, often universalizing them in the process.

According to Barbara, Susan, the winner of so many skirmishes in her long campaign against oblivion, had left no instructions about a "final resting place." Surviving loved ones are now discussing her passion for Balzac and should they bury her near him in the Père Lachaise cemetery at Paris. If they do, I don't envy them all that bureaucratic French paperwork. As it turned out, Susan was admitted to the Montparnasse cemetery where she will join Sartre and Beauvoir, not too bad for a graduate of Hollywood High.

"What?" In front of me on the desk is a copy of *Palimpsest: A Memoir*, published in 1995 and dealing with my first thirty-nine years. I've just read the opening pages, curious to see how I had dealt with the all-important problem of memory. Or is it how memory deals with me? I read: "I have always been curious to know where writers are physically situated when they write memoirs. Their placement during works of the imagination is less relevant because the true geography of a fiction is all in the mind but a memoir is set off by a thousand associations, even by objects in a given room." At the moment, today, in front of me there are several novels by James Purdy on the desk. I've been writing about him, and wondering why so unique a writer has been so ignored. But then, "unique" will do it every time hereabouts. Nearby, a volume of Montaigne's essays, the ultimate touchstone for anyone trying to recollect himself as well as others.

I resist opening Montaigne for as long as possible. I spent an hour once in his sixteenth-century Gascon tower and saw the same view that he saw from his third-floor study window. But where he tells us he had his chicken run, there are now ducks at ground level. Otherwise, inside that round tower room, one can imagine oneself inside his head, preserved in this room as his attempts—essays—inhabit his books. Unable to resist, I turn to the page where he frets about his poor memory. "I am so outstanding a forgetter that, along with all the rest, I forget even my own works and writings. People are constantly quoting me to me without my realizing it." Since I am now thirteen years older than the author of *Palimpsest* and since most of my contemporaries are vanishing, I am often drawn to Montaigne on the subject of memory and its lapses, not to mention on our common mortality. He is surprisingly sardonic on this last delicate subject: "Everybody goes out as though he had just come in," he writes. "Moreover, however decrepit a man may be, he thinks he still has another twenty years." Hardly a delusion of mine as I examine a new cancer on my forearm, all the while waiting for diabetes to do its gaudy final thing. I sometimes imitate Montaigne when he notes that: "I have adopted the practice of always having death not only in my mind but on my lips." Hence, Susan; I am told that a failed marrow implant, not to mention a harrowingly painful chemotherapy procedure, ended her ordeal. Since "each man bears the entire form of man's estate," as Montaigne puts it, I can take part, at a near-remove, in her now abandoned estate so like that of all the rest ever born.

I grow homesick when I read where I was in 1992, my workroom in Ravello: "a white cube with an arched ceiling and a window to my left that looks out across the Gulf of Salerno toward Paestum; at the mo ment, a metallic gray sea has created a white haze that obscures the ever more hostile sun." As I quote these lines I will myself back to then where Howard is still alive and our world has not yet cracked open.

Where am I now? I am in a second-floor study that an old friend, Diana Phipps, copied from a picture of Macaulay's book-lined study. Through the windows in back of my chair, a steady monsoonlike vertical rain has been falling for days, rattling the straight palm trees that hide the road which crosses over from Hollywood to the San Fernando Valley.

I have also just found the deed to the house; apparently, I bought it March 24, 1977, not long after we had bought the villa La Rondinaia ("The Swallows Nest") in Ravello. We moved back here after a routine physical examination; our doctor showed me the X-ray of Howard's chest: at the top of the right lung was a round object like an eyeball with glaucoma, startlingly white against the black foil of the radiogram. A lifetime of smoking had finally done its work; every attempt to stop the addiction had failed and continued to fail. Even after two "successful" cancer operations, he kept right on smoking and that is how "we" ceased to be we and became "I."

To my left, as I write this at the partners desk, there is a chair that bars entrance from the study to the door to Howard's room. Norberto, our Filipino housekeeper, has placed in the chair a puppet Mephistopheles with a white skull-like head and pointed mustache—to ward off the evil eye? But surely that eye has already failed to do its work.

The books here in Macaulay's study are neither mine nor his, alas, but those of an old friend who has finally gone back East. Apparently, during his Western hegira, he had acquired every Literary Guild book club choice of the last thirty years. They are now stacked in the glass-fronted bookcases until my reference books come from Italy . . . if I decide actually to live in a so-called "homeland" daily grown ever more repressive.

I see that a writer in this morning's *Los Angeles Times* chides Sontag for not telling *all* to everyone about her affairs with so many fascinating

At work in the La Rondinaia studio with a white cat waiting for me to thank her for the splendid rat that she has just delivered.

women. Rousseau made the same complaint of Montaigne who was equally reticent about his private life. In the decades that I knew Susan slightly I was dimly aware of her private life and had no interest in it—nor anyone else's for that matter unless it was, in some way, comical. I was also not particularly interested in her meditations on subjects like photography. What did matter to the non-specialized world was her views on war and peace in the Balkans and on the civil war in the Middle East where she sometimes offended the right people. That's enough of death for now.

I've just switched off the television with its endless images of the floods in Southeast Asia. I think fondly of all the winters that Howard and I spent in Bangkok at the Oriental Hotel when it was still just a single high-rise building at the edge of a dark Klong. The manager was a young Swiss married to a Thai girl. I've not been back for several years but I am told that the two of them are still there, if somewhat emeritus. They also presided over the glamorous remodeling some years ago.

EIGHT

———————— ✳ ————————

Outside my windows here, the familiar clatter of rain on palm fronds transports me to Bangkok. The monsoon is early, I think, moving backward in time. I must get dressed for lunch with Crown Princess Chumbhot. Presently—I'm in past time now—I shall leave the W. Somerset Maugham suite where I stay in the old section of the hotel, while Howard is in the new tower. Many suites are named for writers who have stayed in the hotel or its predecessor, starting with Joseph Conrad. Neither of us has ever stayed in the Gore Vidal suite with its view of a series of Klong-side cement factories bedecked with orchids.

We meet in the lobby. A hotel car takes us to lunch through heavy traffic. My mood lightens. Better to be back there in memory than linger here in fact. "Let the dead past bury its dead," as my grandfather used to intone with measured glee as he gradually took up final residence in that very same past as I am now trying to do.

In the sixties, we acquired a new friend in Bangkok, the old Crown Princess Chumbhot, a tiny woman whose palace looks to my Western eye like no more than several highly polished teakwood boxes gleaming side by side in a sunny garden. Since one must never physically tower over a Thai royal, she had placed a series of stone steps beside her front door where she could station herself in a sort of pulpit and thus greet, sublimely, from above, Western visitors. Her father had been Thai ambassador to London where she had gone to school. She spoke with an Edwardian English accent not to mention wit.

Whenever we arrived at the Oriental, the hotel would alert her and she would then invite us to lunch with various interesting folk both Thai and *farang*, as foreigners are known. Apropos our last lunch I got two advance calls from the Crown Princess (she had married what was to have been a king of Thailand, thus making her Crown Princess; when her husband was passed over for the succession, she retained her title).

"I was very remiss," said the cool voice on the telephone. "I had asked a few people to our lunch but then I quite forgot to tell you who they are." I said I'd be delighted no matter who . . .

"Don't speak too soon," she said. "One of the guests is a *fellow* author, a Mrs. Barbara Cartland." I was overjoyed. The ongoing pleasure of Bangkok is that people you don't know, but don't mind observing if only briefly, keep showing up. I reassured our hostess that I was ready for Mrs. Cartland who was famous for her splendid costumes, intricate wigs, dramatic makeup, Rolls-Royces, and innumerable romantic novels about well-born virgins, male as well as female. A Cartland law of matrimony insisted that the bride be totally virginal and inexperienced on her wedding night while, simultaneously, her groom must be equally virginal *but* experienced. Millions of Cartland fans were known to debate this contradiction with Talmudic zeal. Later, at lunch, the author herself joined in the debate. "After all, an experienced older lady *could* have contributed, in the purest way, to the hero's education." This was cryptic, to say the least. Mrs. Cartland was also currently celebrated as the mother of Lady Diana Spencer's stepmother and so, in the eyes of the tabloids, an authority on the royal family whom she ceaselessly defends in the press even when they are not under attack. Recently she had objected to hints in the press that her *dearest* friend, Admiral the Lord Mountbatten, late Viceroy of India, had had perhaps too great an interest in the welfare of navy lads. She was also outspokenly anti-American because she believed that we had not sufficiently aided England in World War Two. Chumbhot was looking forward to a few decorous fireworks at table.

Howard and I arrived for lunch with a relative of the hotel manager's wife; she was another British-educated Thai lady attached to the court. Chumbhot was waiting for us in her stone pulpit. She led us inside where, suddenly, the Thai lady, no young woman, promptly dropped onto all fours in front of Chumbhot who stood very straight like an effigy to herself. The lady then proceeded to writhe like some beached crab across the floor until she arrived at Chumbhot's feet. Then, limbs intertwined, she slowly rose. For a moment I feared that she was going to levitate like Saint Teresa who was so famous for her levitations that the Pope sent for her. But then, just as she was entering his presence, she began uncontrollably to rise in the air, higher and higher. "Oh, Lord," she cried, "not now, not now!" But at the Crown Princess's gesture, the court lady remained earthbound. Also on hand for lunch was Chumbhot's nephew, the architect Tri, whose Royal Yacht Club Hotel has apparently been swept away by the tsunami.

Since Bangkok traffic was the worst in the world in those days, one is never on time. But Mrs. Cartland, stepgrandmother to the new Princess of Wales, arrived more than two hours late. Chumbhot was royally gracious but seething. The heat of the day, despite fans in the sitting room, did not improve the general mood. But should Cartland misbehave Chumbhot and I had prepared a trap.

While waiting for Cartland, Chumbhot and I talked of Kukrit Pramoj who had been prime minister during many of the bad years of the American war in Vietnam, where he maintained a kind of suave neutrality despite his dislike of our crude imperialism not to mention his simultaneous Thai edginess about the Communist empire to the north, the China of Mao Tse-tung. Kukrit also published a major newspaper while supervising a dance company that he'd founded in order to preserve ancient Thai dances. He had, with brio, played the part of a prime minister in *The Ugly American*: "It was bliss," he reminisced. "One rests in an air-conditioned trailer, unavailable for a real prime minister, and one's hair is constantly trimmed, no matter how sparse." He was amused by his co-star Marlon Brando.

The Thai royal family number in the thousands and are ranked according to which king they descend from: Rama One or Two or Three and so on. Kukrit and Chumbhot liked to quarrel over which of the two was the most royal. The current king is revered by all and treated like a living god, even by the sharp-tongued Kukrit who always spoke respectfully of his kinsman though less admiringly of the beautiful queen and her plastic surgeons. Apparently, one day during the Vietnam War, the queen called out some units of the army in the northeast of the country and went to war on her own against Communist rebels. It was said that her troops had also leaked over into Laos. Somehow or other, Kukrit persuaded the warrior queen to come home and peace was restored.

Since Thailand, also known as Siam, has never been conquered or colonized by Europeans, it has developed a society unlike any other in Southeast Asia. There are no resentments of the European powers or the "white race." The Chinese, of course, are regarded with a somewhat beady eye while Kukrit liked to repeat an old Thai saying: "If you are in the jungle with only a stick to defend yourself and you are suddenly approached by an Indian and a cobra, kill the Indian first." But diplomacy and subtlety are the principal Thai weapons of defense; and so they kept the American war party at a distance during the Vietnam episode.

Chumbhot said, "Is it true that Mrs. Cartland was not invited to the wedding of Prince Charles and Lady Diana?" How well I thought the late Truman Capote could have handled all this. He lived for gossip and he was also a marvelous liar. No fact ever gave him pause. When truly inspired, like Joan of Arc attending to her voices, he would half shut his eyes and start inventing stories about people whom he had often never known or, indeed, even heard of. Although he felt himself to be the heir to Proust, a reference I once made to Madame Verdurin drew a blank. I saw him perhaps every other decade, usually by accident. Jackie Kennedy, whom he claimed to have known since childhood, actually met him at a lunch in New York just before the 1960 election. Truman had spun a number of fantastic stories to a table of bemused ladies. At the end of lunch, he asked Jackie if she had a car and, if so, could she drop him off on her way home? She had. She did. In the car, he gave a great dramatic sigh. "Now you've seen me singing for my supper!" He became Pagliacci. Since Jackie had enjoyed him, I warned her, "Just remember all those scurrilous stories you found so interesting about other people he'll now start to invent about you." Luckily, Jackie was never innocent about the Capotes whom she regarded as so many denizens of a zoo which she liked occasionally to patronize. When Jack and Jackie moved to the White House, her stepsister observed that, "This will be the most disdainful administration in history."

Chumbhot is waiting for my answer. Am I to turn Capote-esque? "No," I said, "Mrs. Cartland was not invited." I recalled Princess Margaret, cigarette holder in one hand, a gin and tonic in the other. It was her gift to extract some joy from whatever hand, no matter how bad, life had dealt her. "Of course we were going to invite the old thing," she said, "but the bride's family said that if *she* came, *they* wouldn't and since you can't have a wedding without a bride . . ."

Finally, Mrs. Cartland, escorted by an amiable grown son, made her entrance on a sudden gust of hot air from the garden. As tribute to the heat she wore neither hat nor wig, only wavy tufts of pale hair adorned her gleaming rosy pate.

"*The traffic!*" Cartland was accusing.

"Good afternoon." Chumbhot was demure. In Bangkok, "The traffic!" is almost a greeting. A stickler in print for etiquette, preferably royal, Mrs. Cartland did not curtsey to Chumbhot, so different from the court lady's beached-crab number: *Autre temps* as E. Nesbit's Psammead liked to murmur at such moments. Mrs. Cartland and son were

apparently in the neighborhood in order to check on the distribution of
her books throughout Southeast Asia, a formidable task, they sighed,
considering her alleged popularity.

In the dining room. I sat on Chumbhot's left, Mrs. Cartland, a mon-
ument draped in damp pastel colors, on her right. Conversation did not
flag. Mrs. Cartland was indignant at the way the press had been treating
"Dickie." Dickie Mountbatten. "All this nonsense about his . . . private
life. Perfect nonsense! And then they *dare* to write about Nehru and Edwina [this was Lady Mountbatten], too vile, really." Mrs. Cartland was
beginning to shake with indignation. I couldn't help but think that if
the diarist of that period, Chips Channon, was reliable in these matters
the press was surprisingly accurate and rather mild. What was common
knowledge in a certain world was plainly not to be shared with Mrs.
Cartland's virginal readers. Chumbhot, who knew the same gossip that
the press was working from, said, innocently, "Have you no laws in England to protect the royal family? Don't you have . . . what is the
phrase?" She turned to me.

"*Lèse-majesté*, which you have in Thailand," I added.

"Yes, we do. But what, Mrs. Cartland, do the English do to journalists who attack the Queen?"

"Since Her Majesty does nothing but good, they never do."

I turned to Chumbhot. "What do they do to the press in this country?" was my contribution.

"Oh, I think we still kill them." This made for a more serious mood.
As Mrs. Cartland restlessly stirred her soup, she began on the American
influence on the British press, getting it somewhat backward, I thought.
She expressed outrage that Charles and Diana were being persecuted by
the press when she had never seen a more loving devoted couple. She
was, she confessed, very close to them and knew how hurt they were
with the press telling ridiculous stories about them. "From that glorious
moment in the abbey when they were pronounced man and wife, the
troubles began in our press. Or, I should say, the American press."

Chumbhot picked up our previously agreed-upon cue. "How lovely the abbey must have been. We saw it only on television, of course, but *you* were there." She smiled her gentle tiger smile. Cartland stammered "Yes yes yes . . . then to read in the dreadful press—"

"Do tell us what the abbey was like, with the divine music, the service . . ."

Mrs. Cartland was having trouble with a quail's egg. She coughed and cleared her throat. Chumbhot looked at me. I nodded, "Go!"

"You *were* there?" she asked directly.

"Well, it *was* for *young* people, really. So I gave away my tickets—"

"Surely," said Chumbhot, "the revered Queen Mother is hardly in her first youth." And so it went but not before Mrs. Cartland, perhaps suspecting an American plot, described the inadequate military materiel that the United States had sent to poor beleaguered England, fighting its lonely battle to save civilization. "I know. I was there for Lord Beaverbrook. He taught me how to write. He would have me go down to the docks as those shoddy insufficient arms arrived." Definitely a hot day in Bangkok.

NINE

——————— ✳ ———————

No sooner do I vow to put death, at least temporarily, on that prover-bial back burner than I learn that my coeval, television's Johnny Carson, has died at seventy-nine of emphysema. I was a few weeks older than he. He had rung me last month to say that he had been living pretty much in seclusion at the beach and had only just heard that Howard was dead. We reminisced about his visit to us in Rome and Ravello, a first (and I suspect last) visit to Italy for him. He was not one for foreign climes other than Wimbledon and tennis. In Italy he was a dutiful sightseer but as we climbed Palatine Hill, "Everything here is steps," he sighed, "and broken marble. This place is going to sink under their weight one of these days."

What would Montaigne have thought of him? Had he been a mere entertainer-interviewer, nothing at all. But since Montaigne was deeply interested in politics, Carson would have interested him very much. John was the only political satirist regularly allowed for thirty years on that television time which is known to be prime and so he was able to influence the way the people at large thought about many things that were often unexamined in the media until he put his satiric spin to them. Montaigne wrote to influence the kings of France and Navarre and so was heeded in a way that the performer Carson was also able to influence, in a much smaller way, American politicians. He once told me that he could predict the winner of any approaching presidential election by the reactions to certain jokes he'd tell to the live audiences at his Burbank studio. He'd make amiable fun—at least it *seemed* amiable— of the entire field but all the time that sharp ear was listening carefully to the laughter and, even more attentively, to the silences. He read this microcosm of the American people like a barometer.

What was he really like? Well, he was better looking than he looked. Clowning distorts regular features and his were most regular. The eyes were sharp but the most powerful of his senses was that of hearing, detecting false notes and the lessening of an audience's attention during a joke. The monologue that opened each evening's *Tonight Show* was carefully written out on long rolls of paper that were unfurled as the monologue got read, and the roll of abandoned script would then float from the stage down into the audience where, like Chinese paper dragons, one could read what he had often abruptly cut on air. The face in repose was as composed as that of Buster Keaton if not as comically frozen. One night in Ravello, after his wife Joanna had gone up to bed, we sat on the balcony overlooking the Gulf of Salerno and talked politics and comedy and got quietly drunk.

"You know," he said, "people keep thinking I am this kindly little old Irishman when I'm not little, not kindly, and not Irish but English." Finally it was that ear, sharp to nuance, which directed his performance. We all have multiple responses to what people say particularly if one is on air and must respond quickly. And so, the appearance of amiability is the wisest defense if what you say might break the spell you are spinning. Hence: mock amazement if sex is in the air or wide-eyed bewilderment at a dangerous turn in a political observation. One night before I came out onstage the producer Freddie De Cordova caught me halfway through the curtain: "No mention of abortion; we're having trouble this week!" I said, "All right" and stepped into the spotlight upstage center, then turned right to walk to John's desk where he was unexpectedly beaming. This was unusual. I tried to read his look as I sat in the chair to his right, a swivel chair that tended to slip out from under you in order to face the adjacent couch where other guests might be. "So, Gore, what do *you* think of this right to life movement?" With that, he shoved me into the water, as it were. Offstage, De Cordova looked grim. I started to improvise.

Unlike most talk-show hosts John liked for his guests to be entertaining and so give him a respite from talking as opposed to reacting. Once, in a break, I told him I'd thought of a funny line about someone but I was afraid it might be too sharp. He drummed on his desk with a long pencil and frowned: "If you ever have the *slightest* doubt about a line *don't* say it." The best advice. In front of him just above the camera was a huge clock which, as the minutes passed and guests turned boring, he tended to stare at, waiting to be released from his role. One performance, when he wasn't looking, a member of the crew pushed back the hands of the clock fifteen minutes. Carson's momentary look of despair when he saw the clock got a laugh even though the audience had no idea why.

I first came to his program when he was in a studio on the sixth floor, I think it was, of the NBC building at Rockefeller Center. He had inherited me from his predecessor, Jack Paar, a popular but somewhat eccentric host of *The Tonight Show*.

As we sat drinking on the balcony in the moonlight, we recalled Paar's tantrums and how he had once, in a rage, walked off his own show. Also, how he had asked me if I'd like to be his summer replacement. I had said no. Paar was amazed, but then so was De Cordova who asked me half a dozen times over twenty or thirty years if I'd like to sit in for Carson when he was performing at Las Vegas. "After all," said De Cordova, "when you're in that chair, you're the king." "No," I said. "I may be in the chair but everyone knows that the king is elsewhere. No

John Carson and I warming up on *The Tonight Show*.

thanks." John wanted to know the "real" reason. I said that I had noticed that almost every TV host had written a book that no one wanted to read because they felt that they already knew the author far too well from television to want to know more. So, as a writer for life, I didn't want to lose readers.

It is now time for me to explain what a writer for life—a novelist— was doing on television even though, as of 1962, I had had two success-ful plays on Broadway and was writing films, but not novels.

TEN

————————— ✳ —————————

In World War Two, I was first mate of an army freight-supply ship in the Aleutians. At nineteen, on the long night watches in port at Dutch Harbor, I began a novel set on a ship in the Aleutians—where else? At twenty I was transferred to Birmingham General Hospital in Van Nuys, California: hypothermia—from exposure to the icy Bering Sea—had led to what was misdiagnosed as rheumatoid arthritis. I was offered a lifelong pension if I stayed in the army for another two years (the war had just ended). I said no to the pension if I could be let go right away. Characteristically, on principle, the army held on to me another year and so I became a mess officer at Camp Gordon Johnson on the Gulf of Mexico. After my wisdom teeth were pulled (an eccentric army "cure" for what was finally diagnosed as osteoarthrosis) I was freed. Today I have an artificial knee and no pension. The novel *Williwaw* was published in 1946 to amiable reviews in *The New York Times* and elsewhere. A second novel did less well; a third, *The City and the Pillar*, earned me a letter of congratulations from Dr. Kinsey, himself about to be world famous for his report on the sex life of the human male. But the daily reviewer for the *Times*, a Mr. Prescott, told Nick Wreden, my editor at E. P. Dutton, that not only would he not review my story of a love affair between two "normal" male athletes, but because of the great horror that I had perpetrated in book-chat land he (the most powerful reviewer of the day writing regularly in the daily *Times*) would never again read much less review a book of mine. That was how seven novels of mine went unreviewed in the daily *Times*. Since *Time* and *Newsweek* usually followed the *Times*'s lead, I was neatly erased as a novelist in Freedom's Land. A professor who lectures on my work tells me that academics to this day refuse to believe that the *Times* could ever have done such a thing. Such is simple faith. Happily, England continued to take notice of the books. But, in order to make a living, I turned to one Harold Franklin, an agent at the William Morris office. Since he was more virtuous rabbi than showbiz hustler, he patiently introduced me to live television drama in 1954, where I flourished until branching out into films for Hollywood (as the last contract writer hired by MGM) and from there I moved on to the Broadway stage with *Visit to a Small Planet* and *The Best Man*. I had also found that I enjoyed essay writing, particularly in a recently established publication called *The New York Review of Books*. Finally, by 1964, I was back to novel writing, obliging the aged Mr. Prescott to break his vow and come out of retirement to attack *Julian*, with no discernible effect: his day was done while I had a number of days newly begun. In 1960 I staged a political play on Broadway at the same time I was also the Democrat-Liberal candidate for Congress in New York's 29th District, polling the most votes for a Democrat since 1910 when Franklin D. Roosevelt won a seat in the state senate because so many of the local Republican voters thought that he was his distant cousin Theodore and so voted for him. But once "tricked" they never voted for him again. Since I had practically no money to buy radio time (there was no TV station in the district) for a congressional race, I went on the various national talk shows of which there were at least a dozen. Several insisted that my opponent, the incumbent Republican, be given equal time. Although he'd served several terms as representative to Congress, he had wisely remained unknown to his constituents, secure in the knowledge that the McKinley vote was forever his. He did not go on television, and won. In 1964 I was again offered the nomination but as I was again a novelist I passed the nomination on to Joe Resnick of Kingston who did win. During 1960, I appeared with Jack Paar, Carson, Steve Allen, Merv Griffin: in fact, anywhere that I could get through to the large audience. In the process, I may, also, inadvertently, have changed American publishing. *Julian*, my return to the novel, was not exactly a crackling sexy airport novel: this reflective narrative was about the origins of Christianity and the Emperor Julian's failed attempt to establish religious tolerance in the place of that Christian absolutism installed by his kinsman, Constantine. I had written a book plainly ill suited for raffish bestsellerdom.

In those days publishers were almost as mystified as they are now when it came to the delicate subject of how to lure people into reading books in the age of movies and that upstart, television. Quite by accident, I presented them with a solution. Since I was still thinking about politics in those days, I had continued to go on television whenever possible to talk about the state of the union, which appealed to Carson and a few—very few—other TV hosts. One of the others was Hugh Downs, the low-key star of the *Today* show. In that unhurried time, he and I would sit at a table, *The New York Times* between us, and we'd chat—very low key—about the news of the day with breaks for commercials, weather, solid news. When Little, Brown, the publisher of *Julian*, asked me if I'd go to Houston to Brown's bookstore to promote the book I said it seemed pointless to me but I would, if they insisted. They gave me a date. I tried to cancel because it conflicted with an appearance on the *Today* show with Hugh Downs. "Why not," asked my editor, "do both? Say something about the book on the show." I explained that we mostly talked politics. "So make an exception," I was told. I did. I talked very briefly about the book while Downs held it up like the Grail. Then

I left the studio for the airport and flew to Houston where Ted Brown of the eponymous bookstore said, "Not only did that TV show sell out every copy that we had in stock, but it looks like every copy in Houston is gone, too, all in one morning." *Julian* promptly became the number-one bestseller on the New York *Herald Tribune* list (*The New York Times*—ever consistent—listed it farther down their list but then, some years later, they miraculously kept my *Lincoln* at number two for a couple of years when it was number one in *Publishers Weekly*). Anyway, the rest is publishing history as publishers drove their writers onto television programs, more happy than not to get so much airtime illuminated free of charge. In time, of course, Gresham's not Grisham's law obtained and people got tired of novelists telling how, although their powers of invention were truly extraordinary, absolutely *everything* in their fiction was absolutely *True* and had really happened to them exactly as described. Capote even claimed to have invented a non-fiction (*sic*) novel about an actual murder case.

So—what made Carson himself laugh? Words, not surprisingly. He used them carefully and listened carefully to the way others used them. The moment we realized that we were, somehow, on each other's wavelength was when I was doing my deep hollow-voiced radio-announcer Nixonian voice. I quoted from Nixon's book *Six Crises*: "President Eisenhower was a far more *sly* and *devious* man than people suspected and I mean those words in their very best sense." On air, I got a look of genuine astonishment from John. Then he nearly slid out of his chair. Over the years, when one or the other of us would characterize someone as "sly" and "devious," the other would add in an oily voice, "I assume you mean those words in their very *best* sense."

Last winter I ran into Janet De Cordova, now a widow. She had tried to get John to come to a memorial service for Freddie and he'd said, "I'll think about it." He did. He rang her back and said, "No, I can't do it." When reminded of their long friendship and so on, he was to the point: "I can't do it because everyone thinks I'm still Johnny Carson but I'm not anymore. I wouldn't even know how to fake it. So, I won't be there but I know what a lousy businessman Freddie was and I'll bet his affairs are in a mess so I'm sending you something useful." He sent her a large check and she was pleased. But how odd it must be *not* to be the self you have spent a lifetime perfecting. To vanish like Prospero into thin air, leaving behind pale understudies but no replacement.

As I was writing these last thoughts on Carson, a friend sent me an old clipping which John would have enjoyed. I start to imagine we are back on his show. I remark how the administration is praising the recent election in Iraq where, perhaps, 72 percent voted. I sit in the swivel chair to his right, an old bit of newspaper clipping in one hand.

"I hear, Gore, you've got the latest news from the election in Iraq. It was certainly a real triumph for freedom and democracy, wouldn't you say?" To myself I mutter, "In the very best sense of those words." Aloud I say, "Well, actually, it's from *The New York Times* of September 3, 1967."

"A dicey year for freedom, wasn't it?"

I read the headline: "U.S. encouraged by Vietnam vote: Officials cite 83 percent turnout despite Vietcong terror . . . A successful election has long been seen as the keystone to President Johnson's policy of encouraging the growth of constitutional processes in South Vietnam." Suddenly, we are sitting on the balcony in Ravello.

CARSON

What's that phrase you use all the time for the country?

VIDAL

The United States of Amnesia.

CARSON

I'll open with that, then you read off the "latest" Iraq election news with the quote from 1967.

VIDAL

But where do we do this?

CARSON

Oh, we'll find a show.

VIDAL
>   There isn't one. Remember? *You're* dead.

CARSON (evasively)
>   No, no. I'm just living down at the beach, I think it's called in
>   seclusion.

The screen is now crowded with Leno *et al.* telling jokes until mortar fire drowns them out, and we have faded to black. Anyway, a few of us once heard the chimes at midnight and were the better for it.

ELEVEN

———————— ✳ ————————

I read somewhere how odd it was that although I ran for public office twice I have never really written about either race or, indeed, *why* I ran. Well, part of the why of 1960 was Jack Kennedy who had married Jackie whose mother had taken the place of my mother as Mrs. Hugh Dudley Auchincloss. After my mother and I had moved out of Auchincloss's Virginia house Jackie's mother and sister moved in while my half brother and half sister became Jackie's stepbrother and stepsister. So many divorces and remarriages in our interconnected family has made for numerous weird connections as well as non-connections: I have four stepbrothers, sons of my mother's last husband, General Olds: I have not only never met them but I don't even know their names. Oh, what a tangled web is woven when divorcées conceive.

In 1956 Adlai Stevenson, the Democratic nominee for president, decided to throw the convention open in order to choose a vice presidential candidate. Jack, the junior senator from Massachusetts, placed himself at center stage, battling with Estes Kefauver, a Tennessee senator with a record for fighting crime. When Jack lost, I wrote him a note congratulating him on *not* being Stevenson's running mate since that eloquent figure was clearly not going to beat Eisenhower; and did not.

As Jack began his long campaign for the Democratic nomination for president, I decided to help out with a play called *The Best Man* whose successful run on Broadway did him no harm. Some years later, I wrote another political play, *An Evening with Richard Nixon*: in this case my Nixon character, wonderfully played by George Irving, spoke only Nixon's actual recorded words; this decision to use his actual words as recorded over the years cost me more money in research than I was ever to make out of the play. But with Irving as Nixon the result was wildly comic because Nixon seemed to have no conscious mind. He said whatever was milling about in his overwrought subconscious. In speeches he often turned to Pat, his wife, loyally seated nearby, and, shaking his finger at her, he would intone, "We here in America can no longer stand pat." The producer, an old friend, suddenly succumbed to a fit of megalomania: instead of opening at a small theater like the Booth where my *Visit to a Small Planet* had done so well, he opened *Nixon* at the Shubert, a vast theater that only something the size of *Oklahoma!*, the musical—or indeed the state—could ever have filled. Needless to say, as always, in Nixon land, there were death threats for many of us, while *The New York Times* outdid itself by headlining the review: "A play for radical liberals," certain death for a Broadway play. Actually the play was a sharp preview of Watergate, already unfolding in the wings. A dance critic, Clive Barnes reviewed the play which had done well with tryout audiences. Clive conceded that it was very funny but, by the third paragraph, he knew that he was supposed to attack and did. I think his exact line was: "Gore Vidal has said mean and nasty things about our president." I ran into him not long after and told him, kindly, that in Clive's native England one might refer to "Our" Queen but in the U.S. we never say Our President. The best aspect of the play was a sort of limbo to which George Washington, Dwight Eisenhower, and JFK have been assigned, quarreling with each other as they watch

George Irving (the star), Claire Bloom, and I at the New York opening of
An Evening with Richard Nixon.

with wonder Nixon's inexorable rise to the presidency. As it turned out, aside from revivals, that was to be my last new play on Broadway, made memorable by a young actress who played several different parts. In due course, I became godfather to one of Susan Sarandon's sons by Tim Robbins. Yes: I did say, Always a godfather, never a god.

TWELVE

———————— ✳ ————————

As early as 1959 Judge Joe Hawkins from Poughkeepsie wanted me to run for Congress. Joe was a blue-eyed Irishman with a lively Greek wife. Joe liked show business; he also knew that, thanks to television, I was known to the five counties of the district: Dutchess, Ulster, Greene, Columbia, and Scoharie. Joe was Democratic chairman of Dutchess, the largest county which perversely prided itself on how it had always voted resolutely against its most famous resident Franklin Delano Roosevelt. Now his widow, Eleanor Roosevelt, held sway at Valkill Cottage while the Roosevelt main house was being turned into a museum and the president himself lay buried nearby in the *roosevelt*, Dutch for rose garden.

In 1960 Eleanor wanted Adlai Stevenson to be our candidate again. She disliked Jack because she detested his father nor was she enthralled by Jack's friendship with the Red Scare monger Senator Joe McCarthy. She was dubious about me, too; the increasingly conservative Senator Gore was not a favorite of the Roosevelts. Eleanor did like my father because he was close to Amelia Earhart for whom she had a Sapphic passion that Amelia found disconcerting. Amelia said that Eleanor was always suggesting they make flights together all around the country, just the two of them, communing with the wind and the stars. Although my father maintained that his long relationship with Amelia was simply professional, his sister, while snooping around his bachelor flat in the Anchorage, a small residential hotel on Connecticut Avenue, found in the bathroom a silver-backed hairbrush with the initials A.E. and reddish blond strands of her curly hair in the brush. As a child I longed for Amelia to be my stepmother but nothing came of it. We used to show each other poems that we had written.

In 1960 Jack persuaded FDR Jr., Walter Reuther, and me to be envoys to Mrs. Roosevelt and get her to support Jack for president. We failed: at the Los Angeles convention she was for Stevenson to the end. Once nominated, Jack flew into Hyde Park to woo her. Since Eleanor was nothing if not a realist, she promptly became a partisan. After the election, she sometimes gave me advice to give to him. The first was: "He must get a voice coach. He talks too fast. People can't follow what he's saying." She told me how she herself had had a wonderful coach. Then she gave her sudden high giggle and flashed her Rooseveltian tombstone teeth so like her uncle Theodore's. "Yes, I know my voice is still rather dreadful but it was ever so much worse." She also thought the Kennedy children were in luck. "They will still be so young after eight years in the White House which is no place"—and she frowned grimly— "for young people to be brought up in, where they are flattered and tempted by all sorts of the wrong people." I know that my father was not pleased that young Elliott Roosevelt, the president's son, was going around saying that Gene Vidal was *his* man in the first administration "and so if you wanted an airline route . . ."

Politics. What was the 1960 race about? Overall, the election of 1960 was largely about appearances—literally. In the television debate between Kennedy and Nixon, Kennedy did not look too young as his handlers feared while, sweating on camera and looking ill-shaven, Nixon

I was not present at this meeting between JFK and Eleanor Roosevelt, disguised as a Sherman tank, but I heard from each *fairly* similar stories! Jack looks uncommonly nervous as she encourages him to be like Uncle Theodore and FDR. This was 1961, he has just been elected president. Dallas is two years ahead of him. She died in 1962. R.I.P.

did not appeal to many viewers. The only substantive issue of their joint appearance were two islands off China's shore, Quemoy and Matsu, and were these barren lumps a significant part of the free world to be defended to the death by the United States or simply ignored as they had been throughout history and so hardly worth a third world war. Since Kennedy looked handsome on camera, he won the debates. But tricky Dick Nixon did get one up on Jack. After they shook hands before the debate, Nixon suddenly scowled and pointed his finger accusingly at Jack, making for a stern winning picture of what Adlai Stevenson liked to refer to as Richard the Black Hearted.

Quemoy and Matsu were promptly forgotten and Jack squeaked through to victory, thanks to Chicago's Mayor Daley's sly way with election returns. The country was also being told that we were—all of us—looking for a new generation of young vigorous leaders born in the twentieth century. Dutifully, we pretended that we were. Certainly President Eisenhower did not inspire those of us allegedly eager for new frontiers to cross. In retrospect, Eisenhower managed to keep the peace with a world where Communism was said to be, thanks to the media's shrill warnings, triumphantly on the march everywhere. Although Eisenhower, the general, did not believe that the Soviets were a threat to the United States, he did see them as posing a danger to that commercial free world that we held so dear and so, secretly, he instructed the CIA to overthrow the freely elected Iranian government of Mossadegh who had wanted to tax "our" British oil supply; then the CIA was ordered to overthrow the democratic government of Guatemala because United Fruit did not want to pay any tax at all on "our" bananas that they harvested and sold elsewhere. I'd written a novel about this, *Dark Green, Bright Red*, but in the general blackout of my work it vanished until Castro appeared on the scene and the book was hailed as "prophetic." During the campaign for Congress I reluctantly gave an interview to *The New York Times*, knowing I was being set up because the *Times* did not cover mid-Hudson elections. The interviewer could not stop giggling as he kept repeating, "I know nothing about politics." With the help of Mrs. Roosevelt I had come up with an alternative to military conscription: voluntary service at home or abroad in such places where help was needed. I got such a good response from the district that I passed the proposition on to Jack who adopted it. Once president, it became the Peace Corps headed by his brother-in-law Sargent Shriver. The *Times* interview ignored all real issues except for the one that was supposed to be death to a candidate: recognition at the United Nations of Red China. I found that even the conservative electorate of the mid-Hudson valley were puzzled that we had no relations with the world's most populous country. But Henry Luce, Lord of *Time*, *Life*, and *Fortune* magazines, believed that the great mission of the United States was the Christianization of China. This meant that anyone who favored recognition of their vile regime was promptly smeared as pro-Communist.

In the end, I carried the cities of Poughkeepsie, Kingston, Beacon, Hudson, and Catskill but the McKinley rural vote determined the election. I did get more votes for Congress than Jack got for president, which was satisfying—to me. Jack liked to say that the two humiliations of 1960 were my getting 20,000 votes more than he in upstate New York and Senator Claiborne Pell getting a million more than he in Rhode Island.

Later, he congratulated me on my luck: "Hell, you would have hated the House. I did. It's a can of worms." Joe Hawkins was now eager for me to enter the Senate race against Jack Javits, a Democrat at heart, who wisely ran as a Republican. But he was unbeatable that year. If I'd wanted a serious career in politics I would have run again in 1964 and joined the other worms in the can. But *Julian* had been followed by *Washington, D.C.* and then by *Myra Breckinridge* and I was, as they say, back. By 1982 I had sold the house on the Hudson and got interested in California politics.

THIRTEEN

———————— ✳ ————————

In the twenty-two years since the race for Congress the American political landscape had entirely changed. Issues, never a strong suit in our
politics, were seldom alluded to. Only money—who had raised how
much and from whom—interested the media, and the politicians. Senator Cranston explained the facts of the new politics to me. "Say you're
elected to a six-year term as senator. Say you would like to be elected to
a second term. Unless you sell out to one of the great lobbies, you will
be obliged to raise ten thousand dollars each week for every week of
your first term. That's 312 weeks." This explains why so many senators
are now funded by corporate America. Lately, I gather, the Internet has
made fund-raising somewhat easier and less corrupt but it is a great
burden for anyone who would like to be useful to be obliged to ring up
strangers and ask them for money to run for office. It was not something I was ever able to do, and so did not even try. The admirable
Cranston was himself rather good at it.

In the course of the 1982 primary I talked to numerous journalists.

Most were only interested to know how much money I had raised. When I said, accurately, "practically nothing," they concluded that I was not "serious." Yet I was going up in various polls without running many of those TV ads made gratis for me by well-wishers in television. One journalist in San Francisco, Richard Rapaport, had an interest in California history and here is what he wrote some time after the election. During the buildup to the primary, Rapaport: "had been disappointed to watch the varying degrees to which political writers supped on Gore's spectacular repartee and witty commentaries and then go on to question his electoral bona fides. Inevitably, a hugely amusing and news-desk-pleasing campaign appearance would be chilled by the stopper, 'but really Mr. Vidal, are you serious?'

"A writer from the *San Francisco Chronicle* named Randy Shilts billed himself as the nation's first openly gay mainstream newspaper reporter, and he would soon gain immense fame as the author of *And the Band Played On*. This 1988 history of the ravaging AIDS epidemic would ironically and tragically claim Randy within a few years. Somewhat blinded—I felt—by the light of his own coming-out celebrity, Randy had confronted Gore over the fact that he would not declare himself America's first openly gay Senatorial candidate. Gore had asked me to stay on several occasions as he took Randy aside and patiently explained to him that although it was no secret, his sexuality was his own damn business and not a thing gentlemen of his generation comfortably advertised.

"Each time, Randy took it a little more badly, and then took it upon himself to punish Gore with some unnecessarily, pointedly nasty reportage. I had made it my own brief to make sure that Randy understood that his behavior and critique were neither fair nor professional. Several noisy confrontations occurred between Randy and me to little effect. His *Chronicle* stories continued to damage Gore's campaign and helped, I felt, secure the nomination for Jerry Brown."

FOURTEEN

—————— ✳ ——————

Obituary Time. Arthur Miller is dead and I have broadcast five times today to the BBC, to Italy, to everywhere except our native land where he has always been underrated. I praised *The Crucible* as well as his political courage in the McCarthy years. I have been wondering what to call this memoir. Should it be *Between Obituaries*? Those of us whose careers began in the twentieth century are now rapidly fleeing the twenty-first, with good reason.

I first met Miller at Tennessee's flat in New York shortly before *Death of a Salesman* was about to open. Miller had given Tennessee a copy of the play and had come to pick it up. They had little in common except the director Elia Kazan, who had successfully staged *A Streetcar Named Desire* and I think now, in retrospect, ruined Tennessee's play in the interest of Broadway success. Kazan allowed Brando, as Stanley Kowalski, to upstage the play's true protagonist, Blanche Dubois. The audience was mesmerized by Brando and so found Blanche—his foil—somewhat ridiculous. At the time even Tennessee agreed that Brando's appearance in the theater was unique and there was no way that Jessica Tandy could compete with him. She seemed all tics and mannerisms while he was the male principle writ large. Tennessee, who loved glory almost as much as his inventions, made no fuss then or later.

With the best intentions in the world, Kazan managed to do quite a lot of damage to Tennessee's plays while, simultaneously, making them into sexy melodramatic commercial hits. I think it was that season that someone asked me to define "commercialism" and I said that it is the ability to do well what ought not to be done at all. I admired and personally liked Kazan but I felt the timid Tennessee should have relied on his tricks less and on his own instinct more.

With an Italian playwright, Franco Brusati, I went to Philadelphia to see the tryout of *Cat on a Hot Tin Roof*. In the first scene, Tennessee had written, as a stage direction, that the tension at a gathering of Big Daddy's family, after his recent brush with death at the Ochsner Clinic, is so charged that it is like "a summer storm." As a result of this one note, Gadge had the family arriving during a deafening summer storm with thunder and lightning. Tennessee only sighed. "I have tried to explain to Gadge the nature of metaphor. And failed." Tennessee was always willing to sacrifice aspects of his art to success as represented by Kazan's bold kinetic energy.

During our stay in Philadelphia, Tennessee was persuaded to write an unfunny joke for Big Daddy, played by folksinger Burl Ives. The joke had something to do with an elephant whose genital member was allegedly like that of Big Daddy or was it vice versa? I've forgotten whether or not this "surefire" audience-pleaser stayed in the play but the intended result—a hit—was duly achieved later on Broadway.

Currently, Tennessee and the theater are on my mind because I have, finally, after fifty years, got ready a play called *On the March to the Sea* which was given a "dramatic reading" at Hartford, Connecticut, and then recently at Duke University where we played fourteen performances with a first-rate New York cast. What is a dramatic reading and how does it differ from—well, an undramatic reading? There are no sets, no costumes. The actors (we had nine) sit in a row upstage center. Downstage there are five lecterns. When an actor hears his cue he goes to a previously assigned lectern and opens his script and pretends to read. Actually the play has been learned and rehearsed for a week or so before the "reading." The model for all this was a famous Dramatic Reading years ago of Shaw's *Don Juan in Hell*, with Charles Boyer and Charles Laughton. Mailer revived this staging for himself, Sontag and me, with, admittedly, somewhat different results from the Boyer-Laughton version.

At Duke our director, Warner Shook, also appropriated the form which works particularly well with a play that depends entirely on its language. Also, since there are no sets or costumes, this saves the producers a million or so dollars while making the company easy to tour. Since things went well at Duke the producer expects to keep the "reading" on the move with, one hopes, as many of the original actors as possible, hard to do since they tend to be in demand elsewhere. After certain performances at Duke, my contract called for me to chat back and forth with the audience on whatever happens to occur to us. I find this, as always, enjoyable and the public seems not to mind. As we are in North Carolina, language is a great local skill as it is in most of the South where the play is set in a small town during the Civil War. A half-mad and so half-sane Yankee colonel occupies the town and moves into the house of its leading magnate. Chris Noth played Colonel Thayer and he and the house owner, Harris Yulin, duel with each other as the narrative gets more and more surreal. Are they all dreaming? Or dead? The ending surprises and, I think, satisfies. I found it liberating to be writing Southern or "Southron" as the play has it. I evoke the cadences and language of my grandparents. Tennessee, a fair poet himself, was drawn to Southron locations because he found the naturalistic American speech of our day ill suited as a basis for poetry of the sort that he liked to evoke in dialogue. And so, deliberately, he mined the speech of his youth, of his Episcopal minister grandfather, of his garrulous metaphor-inclined mother, and of those crippled heroines often based on his sister, Rose, who had un-

Norman Mailer and me with Susan Sontag and Gay Talese in *Don Juan in Hell* to raise money for the Actors Studio.

dergone a barbarous lobotomy; yet even the damaged Rose had a kind of magniloquence: once she mailed him some pot holders that she had made herself with the note, "I have created them in bright tragic colors."

I watched my new play either in the wings on those occasions when I was obliged to speak after the performance to the audience, or in the back of the theater where, by watching the backs of heads, one can tell to what extent a play is holding the audience's attention.

There was one awful price we had to pay for playing in Durham, the heart of the tobacco industry: the occasional uncontrolled thunderous cougher, one of whom nearly brought the production to a halt at the last performance.

Just before I arrived at Duke my nephew Burr Steers, a film director–writer, and I had gone to Rock Creek Cemetery in Washington to bury Howard's ashes in a plot that we had bought some years ago. Barrett Prettyman, a constitutional lawyer, and his wife, as well as Barbara Epstein and the agent Alice Lee Boatwright joined us under a crimson cloth marquee.

The cemetery is vast with great original trees and graves that date back to before the Republic. Three pleasant young women (standing in for the Fates?) placed a metal box in a hole beside the gray marble slab with his name and mine inscribed side by side (his birth-death dates are now complete; mine not—yet). Then we walked over to the Saint-Gaudens statue of "Grief": a partly veiled young man commissioned by Henry Adams in memory of his wife, Clover, who had killed herself. A semicircular seat faces the statue and it was here, Eleanor Roosevelt told me, that she would come and sit when Washington life became particularly unbearable for her.

Henry Adams, our neighbor now in Rock Creek Cemetery, was in life a neighbor of the Roosevelts who lived in the White House across the street from the joint mansion shared by Adams and John Hay, who had been one of Lincoln's secretaries as well as Theodore Roosevelt's secretary of state. Hay had suffered a good deal from that "very embodiment of noise," as Henry James called Theodore.

Here I am next to Saint-Gaudens's Statue of Grief which Henry Adams had commissioned in honor of his wife, Clover. Two or three yards away Howard is buried as I shall be in due course when I take time off from my busy schedule.

As we gathered about the Statue of Grief I recalled the row between Adams and Theodore over the gender of the veiled mourning figure. TR, as he was called by the press, maintained the figure was that of a girl. Adams, who had only commissioned the statue, said that it depicted a young man. TR, never more emphatically in the right than when he was wrong, refused to back down. I have been told that Henry Adams never again crossed the street to visit the first President Roosevelt although he enjoyed TR's cousin Franklin even when he was a mere assistant secretary of the navy.

Eleanor liked talking about Henry Adams. "When Franklin and I were first in town, I would go out in my carriage with all the children, they were very little then, and we would stop in front of Mr. Adams's house and he'd come out and roughhouse with the boys in the back of the carriage. They all had such a wonderful time and even Mr. Adams forgot to be so pessimistic. You know, he'd say things like 'It makes no difference who is president.' Well, it certainly does."

While I recalled this story, Mrs. Prettyman was examining the handsome bare forearms of Grief and pronounced that their size and muscularity indicated that Grief was indeed male.

Jefferson once noted that although he could see the possibilities of some good, even utility, in most human emotions, no matter how negative, he found nothing redemptive or useful in Grief. I thought of that as I looked at the end of the semicircular bench where Howard and I were photographed the day we bought the nearby plot. Howard looks— for him—rather severe. Premonition of *now*? The gossipy biographer who took our picture asked him what he thought, as a Jew, of ending up in so Christian a cemetery: "Amused," he said, and no more. Elsewhere, the writer goes on and on about my fear of death which strikes him, without evidence of any kind, as neurotic. I did point out that no one afraid of death would cheerfully show such a gossip his future grave. I suspect I had probably quoted Montaigne on the subject and this was scrambled in the writing as was so much else that he was told.

FIFTEEN

———————— ✳ ————————

Barbara Epstein tells me that Joan Didion has just written a good book on grief, apropos the recent death of her husband, John Gregory Dunne. I saw her shortly afterward in Los Angeles at a friend's house. We compared notes on the subject. The worst, we agreed, was having no one to talk to as well as the blankness of familiar rooms, lacking their usual occupant. Certainly at one's age there are no substitutes, no replacements, recently attested to by Nancy Reagan: we both attended Sidwell Friends School in Washington at the same time during the thirties but we never knew each other then or, indeed, until quite recently when we joined the ever-increasing company of widows and widowers cluttering Los Angeles. "Don't you hate it," she said, "when they tell you how time is the great healer?" I agreed that I hated it, because, "after all, time is the great constant reminder of things lost and gone for good."

At the grave site the three young women opened a metal box and removed a triangular plastic bag containing brown ashes, which they placed in a hole that had been dug in the yellowy earth next to the marble rectangle. Someone had brought roses and we placed them, one by one, in the underworld at our feet. By then my new knee was growing unsteady and I hobbled back to the car while the Prettymans went to look at Jimmie Trimble's nearby grave. It wasn't until later we learned that this day had been the sixtieth anniversary of the battle for Iwo Jima where, at eighteen, he had been killed.

I've just read in the newspaper how all those marines had been slaughtered to gain possession of an island that proved, in the end, to be of no strategic use to our military. Worse, it was practically impregnable because, unknown (as usual) to our "best" intelligence, the Japanese had dug a series of underground tunnels where twenty thousand troops lay in deadly wait for the invaders. Jimmie's last letters home show how aware he was that they were all being thrown away for no purpose other than the enrichment of war contractors. He also added, bitterly, that "no one will remember what we've done, only how much they made out of it." Since his mother had been secretary to a powerful congressman this sunny apolitical athlete had always had a good idea of just how things actually worked in a country such as ours, nor was he alone: during the three years I spent in the army I never heard a single patriotic remark from a fellow soldier, only grief for friends lost and, almost as often, a fierce grievance felt for those back home who were decimating our adolescent generation.

SIXTEEN

———————— ✳ ————————

I now surrender to Montaigne's request. How did the living die and what did they say and how did they look at the end? Howard has now quietly entered this narrative, as he remains permanently present in my memory.

In 1976 I was elected to the American Academy of Arts and Letters, an august assemblage to which William, but not Henry, James refused to accept election. I also refused the election. When an interested party asked me why I had said "no," I quoted William James who had said that he disliked too many of the inclusions as well as the exclusions. Pressed further, I noted that "I already belong to the Diners Club." This was quoted here and there and, though academy revisionists like to say that I did not *write* this in my letter of rejection, I did *say* it to an official of this congregation of American immortals. A quarter century later, as our millennium was drawing to a close, the president of the academy (my onetime cousin due to marriage who ceased to be my cousin due to a subsequent divorce and remarriage that provided him

with Jackie Kennedy as my replacement), this old friend and esteemed
fellow novelist-historian, Louis Auchincloss, said that it was time that I
behaved responsibly and accepted my ancient election with good grace
since, once elected, one is forever, like it or not, installed on Parnassus.
So I was duly inducted; then a splendid dinner was served. A couple of
dozen fellow academicians and their friends, many of whom I had not
seen in years, filled a large hall outside the dining room with their
wheelchairs, reminding me of the dodgem cars at Glen Echo Amusement Park near Washington, D.C.

Howard and I had just flown in from Italy; we were both tired. Later
that night Howard was ill. Food poisoning? Acute Academitis? The next
day, he was still sick but we flew on to Los Angeles where we stayed at
the Beverly Hills Hotel as our house was not ready. It was a weekend
which meant that all the doctors we knew were playing golf. Finally,
we tracked one down on the golf course and he prescribed medicine for
us at a pharmacy that would not fill his prescription without at least
a notary public's seal. Thus, we entered the ongoing bureaucracy of
American medicine, never again to be avoided this side of Rock Creek
Cemetery. Fortunately, we were covered by insurance but, even so, catastrophic illness still manages to be endlessly expensive.

Howard was now running a fever; his bowels were not working; and
he had a terrible pain across the upper abdomen which was tight as a
steel band. Plainly, it was appendicitis. Fortunately, the hotel had a
young intern on call who took one look at Howard and said, "I'm taking him to the emergency room at UCLA Hospital." Then an old friend,
Wendy Stark, came to the rescue. She knew all the doctors at UCLA
where her father, Ray Stark, a movie producer, was a benefactor. By now,
Howard was feverish and seriously ill. I told the doctors that he had
every symptom of appendicitis, which I had had. Patiently, it was explained to me that no one at seventy could have a functioning appendix, much less appendicitis. Until further tests, it was clear that he had
cancer, possibly of the colon. They would do full tests the next day and

did not operate that evening. During the night, the appendix burst and he was suddenly dying of peritonitis. Once medical folklore was dispensed with, a competent surgeon operated. Howard's abdominal cavity was awash with poison which, once drained off, made a slow shaky recovery possible.

We celebrated the millennium at the hotel in rooms on the ground floor. There was something soothing about watching the fireworks all around the world as well as those in the distance beyond the hotel. We talked about living for a time in the Hollywood Hills which we would have to do while he convalesced and I rewrote for CBS my screenplay for *The Catered Affair* which MGM had originally made with Bette Davis. Although everyone I dealt with at the network "loved" the screenplay it seemed I was insufficiently artful in creating the forty-four or so commercial breaks (usually done *after* the film is made). This was the extent of everyone's interest and expertise. In the end, I suggested that they might be better off *not* doing movies at all—I think they may have taken me seriously because for a time they did abandon producing slices of movie filler to separate the commercials from each other, the only object of their peculiar enterprise.

Once Howard was recovered from peritonitis (and duly weakened by so sustained an attack on his immune system), we went back to Italy in the spring of the first year of the new millennium. Howard had a good appetite and slowly recovered in what Norman Douglas once called Siren Land. It was our last contented time at the villa. Later, back in Los Angeles, there had been that routine radiogram, as I have described: more visits to Cedars-Sinai where the splendid Scots surgeon who had taken on the case warned me that if the tumor had spread he would not operate because Howard's other lung was so weakened by emphysema that it alone could not support him.

Once again, I accompanied Howard in his wheelchair along corridors that I was to know eventually by heart. He was now cheerful, a tribute to his sweetness of character since he knew that I was the one mute

Ernest Borgnine and Bette Davis at the end of *The Catered Affair*, my first screenplay under the MGM contract. Bette looks weirdly like my mother. She didn't care for the director who screamed at the grips and whispered thrillingly to Bette while he showed her how to pour coffee from an old pot in the kitchen. "I may not," she said, "be much of an actress, but I am marvelous with props." She said this was her favorite movie of the final phase.

with dread. As the nurse opened the door to the operating room where I could not follow, Howard turned to me in his wheelchair and said, "Well, it's been great." Then the door closed behind him.

I waited in an area near the operating rooms. I watched the clock. One, two, three hours passed. I had a series of waking nightmares. He had died on the operating table. The inadequate lung had given out. All around me people, presumably in my situation, were nursing their own nightmares. At last the surgeon appeared. It had been a long procedure but he had got all the tumor out and much surrounding tissue.

A day later we were celebrating what was, in effect, a "cure": that is, he was free of every sign of cancer in the lungs. One knew that cruel recurrence was the nature of the beast but at least this clean initial sweep was encouraging. We went home to Italy. The white cat and the brown cat, thirteen-year-old brothers, were waiting patiently for us at the gate and, with military precision, escorted us to the villa.

Rita, who works for us part-time, has studied nursing and was helpful as Italians tend to be whenever medical problems arise. One now arose with me. I had foolishly allowed a Roman surgeon to flush out a torn meniscus in the left knee, thus neatly crippling me. I assume the surgeon thought that I'd take the next step and allow him to install an artificial knee but I preferred to suffer pain until I was back in Cedars-Sinai land.

During that lovely last Siren Land spring, Howard fell coming out of the pool. More tests—this time in Naples. Cancer had spread to the brain. We tried to fly back to Los Angeles but were warned that the plane's cabin pressure, at transatlantic altitude, would cause the water gathering in his skull literally to boil. A doctor friend in Rome, although officially retired, still worked at a private Roman clinic. We checked in. An MRI revealed a small dark bubble on the lobe of the brain that controls locomotion. He had also become incontinent. Several times I had to lift his deadweight off the floor until, finally, I ruptured a spinal disk. Donella, our doctor friend, arranged for a distinguished surgeon at Rome's Villa Margherita to operate. But when the professor had studied the MRIs of Howard's brain he said, "We must not wait." Unfortunately a long holiday weekend was coming up and such weekends are sacred in Italy. The operation was scheduled for the next week. As I left Howard's room, he said, "Kiss me." I did. On the lips, something we'd not done for fifty years. When I rang the Villa Margherita the next morning, he was not in his room. The Roman team of doctors had, amazingly, ignored the holiday and he was now in surgery. I waited most of the day and some of the night in a room above the operating room. Finally, in a large elevator shaft, he arrived on a lift from the operating room below. He was naked and unconscious like a corpse in a fifteenth-century painting of the plague years. Attendants carried him into a cell where his vital signs were constantly checked, their lights blinking as intravenous tubes were placed in his arms. One nurse asked me his name and if he spoke Italian. I told him the name and assured him that Howard spoke Italian. The nurse kept calling his name until Howard finally opened his eyes; saw me; winked; went back to sleep. One of the distinguished surgeon's aides told me what a success the operation had been. "Oh, there is still a spot or two," and he mumbled the Italian word for *metastasized*. I had a sudden image of Howard on the bench in front of the Ravello post office where the old men sit in the sun. Then, when one of them dies, they all move down one place toward the main road. He was now close to the corner.

The next day, I began to negotiate for a small hospital plane to fly us to Los Angeles. Meanwhile, we went back to Ravello. Howard had recently begun to hallucinate; luckily, he knew that he was hallucinating so he'd report with some fascination on what he *thought* was going on about him. "Look! They have made this hospital room look exactly like my bedroom in Ravello," he said from his bed in Ravello. "But then in Rome they also pretended that I was still in Ravello even though I could see the sea from my window. You've got to admit the special effects are wonderful." Then good humor would suddenly change to anger at me. "Why is it always about you?" he began to rage apropos nothing that I had said. Worse, despite the success of the operation, he still could not walk.

Finally, the private plane was ready and it was time to go. In the piazza Ferdinando, owner of the bar San Domingo where Howard had sung so many nights over the last thirty years, had got up early to say farewell and to recall all those good times never to come again. Howard listened gravely; spoke briefly; Ferdinando wept.

The hospital plane was like a flying coffin with two nurses, two pilots, Howard, a general assistant from Los Angeles, and me, crippled leg bent under me. We flew to the Azores and I took a shaky walk on the steamy tarmac. Equatorial heat. Howard slept, snoring, from the Azores to Iceland to Indianapolis, as we zigzagged across the Atlantic and North America. Then back to the house in the Hollywood Hills.

More trips through the bowels of Cedars-Sinai. This time to a special radiation room. Howard's head was bolted in place against a piece of metal as the gamma rays were zapped at his skull theoretically knocking out remnants of the original cancer which I could not help but think that the Roman surgeon might have been tempted to excise on his first visit to the site. As always, I was struck by the euphoric good humor of the various oncologists, as cancer specialists are known. Since most of their patients will die more soon than late, they exude a depersonalized charm that is positively presidential in its effect. Howard emerged from the agony of the gamma ray room looking haggard but very much in his right mind. "I don't think I want to do that again," he said as we drove home.

The next few days were sunny and peaceful. He sat outside one Sunday morning reading the newspapers while I sat nearby restoring my novel *Creation* to its original state, undoing a deranged editor's handiwork. "Come up," he said. "And sit here, next to me." I said I would in a minute but in a minute he'd gone upstairs. Then all hell broke loose. He was having heart spasms. An emergency ambulance arrived. Then back to the emergency room at Cedars-Sinai. But it was not a heart attack, only a spasm that had something to do with emphysema. He was now also permanently attached to an oxygen tank. Needless to say, when the tank was switched off, he would, somehow, find a cigarette and puff on it. I made no fuss.

We went through a squadron of nurses, mostly useless. Finally, we got Leto, a sixty-year-old grandfather who looked twenty years old. Leto agreed to a twenty-four-hour vigil sleeping on a sofa beside Howard's hospital bed. Hallucinations were now returning. He always kept asking what day of the week it was, "Because Thursday I'm being let out of here." He had decided that we were both in some sort of governmental hospital prison. When, he wondered, would I be let go? I said when he was. In the mornings when I'd come into his room, Leto would be tidying him up and Howard would follow me with his eyes as if trying to fix me in his memory.

Next he developed pneumonia and Edward, a Russian nurse—actually an M.D. but not allowed to practice in the United States except as a nurse (disgusted, he went to an American law school and gave up medicine for law)—would come at dawn to plug Howard into antibiotics. One morning Howard announced to me in near-pentameter, "At first light the angel of death, all in white, arrived with the sun."

Montaigne would now want to know how he looked. He had good color. An excellent appetite. A television set was almost always on—for Leto. Howard was ranking the commercials according to which ones he most hated.

A sort of swinging cage had been set up above his hospital bed and he was lifted in it as Leto cranked until he was able to swing him from bed to an armchair where he could sit and look out the window at tall trees as well as at a datura bush growing on the next property; he also had a view of the Italianate tile roof of the garage apartment opposite.

Each midnight he would start to sing. Leto, who had been a piano prodigy in Manila, would accompany him on the downstairs piano. He pronounced Howard's voice better than Andy Williams's, which it was. Howard had sung professionally until he realized, sadly, that he was a minor latecomer to that golden age of male singers, headed by Frank Sinatra and Tony Bennett. Unlike most of the great stars higher up the list, Howard never lost his voice though emphysema was reducing volume. He had worked in advertising before we met, putting himself through New York University by working eight years at Walgreens drugstore next to the Paramount Theater in Times Square. He still sang; he had a repertoire of several hundred songs and despite all the recent surgeries and hallucinations he never forgot a lyric. Cole Porter, Sondheim, and his favorite "Our Love Is Here to Stay" echoed through the house at the end. Also, in Ravello, when he couldn't sleep, he would play Barbra Streisand's final concert which she had invited us to London to attend. He always felt that he had somehow invented her because he'd seen her with me on *The Tonight Show* when she was unknown: she had sung Arlen's "A Sleeping Bee." Not long after her first Carson appearance, we gave a small dinner party in New York to celebrate Paul Newman's fortieth birthday. Howard invited Streisand and we introduced her to Beluga caviar. She never looked back. How did she start her day? interviewers would ask. "With five thousand eggs," she'd reply. We toasted Paul's birthday. "I guess," said Howard, "forty must seem very old to you." "Yes," said the practical Streisand, "it does." So, as Howard was dying he listened over and over again to her last album.

Near the end he asked me, "How old am I?" I told him he was seventy-four. He frowned. "That's when people die, isn't it?" I said that I hadn't and so far he hadn't. I was sitting beside his armchair looking out over the tile roof opposite. For a moment he looked puzzled; then he said: "Didn't it go by awfully fast?" Of course it had. We had been too happy and the gods cannot bear the happiness of mortals. Montaigne paid for *his* wisdom with agonizing kidney stones.

Several times I asked Leto to wake me when Howard began to sing but Leto never did. I suppose, at the end, Howard wanted to do a benefit for himself alone. I can understand this, sadly, because I loved his singing. One winter at the Bamboo Bar in Bangkok's Oriental Hotel he sang regularly at popular request. It seemed all of young Bangkok wanted to hear this heir to Tony Bennett. Then there was a memorable session with the band at Brasilia airport, wonderful musicians who cheered him on as did a crowd of Brazilian parliamentarians, waiting for the weekend plane to take them home to Rio de Janeiro, far from Brasilia, their truly ugly jungle capital.

Leto never did wake me at concert time. With the aid of Valium I was sleeping too heavily, or so he said. Heavy sleep is my own natural response to the unbearable and yet, for most of this time, I had convinced myself that Howard was going to survive indefinitely due to the magic of radiation. But then "Denial," as Bill Clinton once so neatly put it, "is not just another river in Egypt."

During the days we talked of usual matters. Particularly, the presidential threats of war in the Middle East. Howard regretted that in all the years we had spent living outside the United States we had continued to pay, as law required, full income tax to a federal government plainly gone berserk. One of the last public occasions he had been able to attend was my speech at UCLA's Royce Hall where I talked to a thousand people against the coming wars.

At these times, during such an illness, the mind keeps finding new reasons for hope—at least mine did and I think that his did, too; not long before the end he had a serious workout with a physical therapist who found him unexpectedly strong, physically and even more so mentally as he drove himself to rebuild his body.

Logistically, I had a difficult time being alone with him. There was always something Leto had to do—swinging him from armchair to bed and back again, changing the uncomfortable diapers he was obliged to wear. The hospital bed also had a railing around it and one could barely poke a hand through in order to hold his hand. Since we usually watched the evening news together I decided one night that he should stay in his armchair and I'd sit next to him and so we watched together, talking to the screen as much as to each other. When the news was off, he was silent. Leto was out of the room. "Don't you want to talk?" I asked. There was a long silence, then he shook his head.

"Why not?"

"Because," he said, "there's too much to say."

The next morning Edward gave him his intravenous antibiotics. The coughing was still bad from an ominous bout with pneumonia but, as he noted triumphantly, "Green to beige." I was too slow to get this. Exasperated, he said, "What I've been coughing up was green—poison—now it's a beige color, almost healthy." We celebrated "green to beige." The next day the physiotherapist would be back and I vowed that I would not take Valium and so be able to listen to the midnight concert. Leto arrived with his supper which he put on a table in front of the armchair. I went downstairs to get a sandwich. A few minutes later Leto shouted, "Mr. Auster has stopped breathing!" I ran upstairs. He was still in the armchair, facing the window. He had eaten most of his dinner. In front of him was a tin of some vitamin concoction that he liked. Leto said, "He just drank that drink and took a deep breath and then he—stopped." I sat in the chair opposite and did all the things that we have learned from movies to determine death. I passed a hand in front of his mouth and nose. Nothing stirred. Montaigne requires that I describe more how he looked—rather than how I felt. The eyes were open and very clear. I'd forgotten what a beautiful gray they were—illness and medicine had regularly glazed them over; now they were bright and attentive and he was watching me, *consciously*, through long lashes. Lungs, heart may have stopped but the optic nerves were still sending messages to a brain which, those who should know tell us, does not immediately shut down. So we stared at each other at the end. He had been sitting straight up when I came in the room but now, very slightly he slumped to the left in his chair. Leto had gone to ring 911. "Can you hear me?" I asked him. "I know you can see me." Although there was no breath for speech, he now had a sort of wry wiseguy from the Bronx expression on his face which said clearly to me who knew all his expressions, "So this is the big fucking deal everyone goes on about." In my general state of confusion I was oddly comforted that in death he was in perfect easy character much as he would have been that evening if he had lived to sing "New York," the song the people in Ravello often begged him to sing fortissimo.

Jim Carney who works for us at times kept me company while the newly arrived team from 911 hurled him onto the wood floor time and again. If he'd had a spark of life, all that pummeling would have extinguished it. When they finally finished, I thought they were going to take him to whatever hospital they had come from, so I said, "Could you take him instead to Cedars-Sinai, that's his regular hospital." One of the medics said, "He's not going to a hospital, he's going to the mortuary."

Then Jim and I were left with Howard on the floor between us covered by a sheet, black socks on his feet. Leto wept. I envied him—the WASP glacier had closed over my head. It took over an hour for the ambulance to come take him away. During the wait, I pulled back the sheet for one last look at those clear gray eyes—could they still see?—but the substance of the eyeballs had collapsed and two gelatinous streaks of the sort snails make had coursed down his cheeks. I would not see him in any corporal form again until the ashes at Rock Creek Cemetery.

But, curiously, last night I finally saw him clearly in a dream—a frustration dream. We were in a side street in Rome where the entrance to our old flat should have been but was nowhere to be found. Yet everything else was as it should have been, including a greengrocer whom we knew. Howard had grabbed a handful of fava beans and started to shell them. For what it is worth the fava bean itself resembles a miniature fetus and the Pythagorean cult believed that each bean contains the soul of someone dead, ready to be reborn. In the dream Howard was eating these forbidden fetuses—preparing for rebirth?

SEVENTEEN

———————— ✳ ————————

Just as I decided that I was done with obituaries the Pope and Saul Bellow die. The mourning for the Pope seems weirdly irreal. Much is made of the conversions that he is given credit for on the African continent where his stern prohibition of contraceptives has crowded the Catholic heaven with African angels. Meanwhile the media in the United States, as always off the mark, treats him rather the way they did Marlon Brando, another superstar who was also never, as they say, not on.

If Thomas Jefferson had found nothing at all useful in grief, I found it weirdly energizing. Certainly, the aftermath of a death in today's United States brings one into contact with all sorts of strangers: lawyers, accountants, morticians, insurance claimants, not to mention old friends in their thinning ranks and new acquaintances in their thickening ones.

Although I have played parts in a number of films I was never an actual actor and so, except for a school performance of *The Comedy of Errors*, I had never acted on a stage anywhere until some New York producers offered me the lead in *Trumbo*, a play based on the letters of the blacklisted screenwriter Dalton Trumbo. The producers were rotating the part of Trumbo among a number of actors ranging from Richard Dreyfuss to Nathan Lane. After the storm of bureaucratic activity in the wake of Howard's death, all I could think of was flight, in every sense. Work of any kind had always been my best refuge. Why not appear on-stage for a week or two at the Westside Theater? I could never memorize in youth but *Trumbo* is a series of letters that he wrote, often to his son played onstage by Gordon MacDonald. There was, happily, no director by then, only an excellent stage manager and a workable set where I would make my entrance in near-fatal darkness back of screens showing film footage of the various disturbances of the 1940s when Dalton Trumbo fell afoul of congressional Red hunters with his sharp responses to their deeply un-American catechisms. For a long time while Trumbo was officially blacklisted by the Hollywood establishment, he wrote scripts under pseudonyms as well as many letters which I enjoyed performing. I had known Trumbo slightly in Rome where he had invited me to his splendid apartment overlooking the Tiber: he wanted to talk to me about the Byzantine Empire: the background to a movie he was writing for an Italian producer. He was obviously being well paid and I thought of the pluses of *not* having one's name on a script particularly in an era like today's when "focus groups" examine one's every line for inadvertent lack of political correctness or its somber incubator unwanted originality. In the end I had the impression that Trumbo was enjoying his well-paid martyrdom not to mention special status since, as he liked to point out, nearly every distinguished film covertly made abroad was credited to him while the disasters— some of his own making—remained parentless. Finally, he was white-listed again and the Oscar awarded to one of his pseudonyms was finally presented to him. All in all a curious time. Whatever his talents as a dramatist he was a marvelous letter writer as I discovered reading them to appreciative audiences: he was witty, often wise, and sometimes moving. I played him seated at center stage. To my left were, always for some reason, the heavy laughers, to my right the more subdued listeners. Performance after performance the laughers found their preordained seats and the others theirs. Early on I had problems with one speech: a letter to the mother of a young man who dies in the war: Trumbo had been in the Pacific theater with him. He writes the mother a letter which, invariably, brought me to tears whenever I read it. Since the first law of acting is let the audience not the actor do the weeping, what to do? I finally got a pin so that whenever my voice quavered during the reading of the letter, I would stick it in my thigh and thus, distracted, betrayed nothing until the night when the audience to my right, always so reliably attentive, was silent: Had I lost them? A large woman on the front row started up the aisle. Were they *leaving*? Mild panic. Afterward, I asked the stage manager, "What went wrong?" He told me that the lady who had gone up the aisle was one of the producers who had seen half a dozen actors play Trumbo and she was sobbing. So was much of the right-hand side of the audience. As a hardened public speaker I knew how to make an audience laugh. But never before or since had I made one weep.

On the night when many of the actors in town come to see a play, I saw most of the cast of the recent revival of *The Best Man* as well as Elaine May and her gentleman friend Stanley Donen whom I knew from our days at MGM. Afterward, Elaine at her most Mayish, said: "I didn't know you could do this." "You never asked," I was modestly precise. Stanley who had been making musicals at MGM for years before, during, and after the blacklist summed it up: "What you've done is prove that you can act, but the big surprise is that Trumbo could write." There we were, freezing backstage, marooned in 2003 and it was like the great studio was still functioning and all was right with the world and, presently, Arthur Freed will find a musical for Donen to do and Elaine is still doing comic impressions with Mike Nichols while I . . . There are these strange slips in time, away from bleak present to a past present where everyone is suddenly what they were and the dead live.

EIGHTEEN

———————— ✳ ————————

In Rome I usually found the Jesuits not only congenial but often wise. Not long after Karol Wojtyla, Archbishop of Kracόw, was raised by the Holy Spirit to the See of Peter as John Paul II, the Jesuits were ready with a joke. The new Pope addresses God: "Almighty, will there be a married clergy in my time?" "No, my son, not in your time." "Almighty, will there be women priests in my time?" "No, my son, not in your time." "Almighty, will there be another Polish Pope?" And God bellows: "*Not in my time!*" The Jesuits had done their homework. All the potential reforms that had come out of Vatican II were sternly undone by a fourteenth-century Prince-Bishop from Poland primarily interested, like Pius IX before him, in papal authority based on the most literal illiberal readings of Scripture. The result has been a serious shortage of priests in the United States with ever fewer would-be priests on the horizon while the parishioners pick and choose which of the Pope's commands to obey and which to ignore; meanwhile, Brazil's huge

Catholic majority is splintering off into strange protestant evangelical groupings.

But watching the crowds in Saint Peter's Square night after night was for me a nostalgic trip in time. I first set foot in the piazza in the summer of 1939. The heat was Washingtonian. The Pope then was Pius XII, now generally thought to have been too accepting of the Hitler regime. Years later when Howard and I were living in Rome's Via Giulia, Pius XII (real name Pacelli) finally died. Apparently, he was something of a faddist when it came to medicine. The ultimate fad proved to be his embalmment by what seems to have been an amateur taxidermist. As a result, while he lay in state in the basilica, he turned, according to one viewer, "emerald green." Then, in response to the summer heat, he suddenly exploded. This was kept from the world for a long time until someone (a Jesuit?) passed on the information. It is also reported that many sturdy Swiss guardsmen fainted during this holy combustion.

Although an absolute nonbeliever I saw the church as a fascinating shadow of imperial Rome with its curia so like the Roman Senate whose building is still pretty much intact in the Forum.

NINETEEN

———————— ✳ ————————

From time to time, Saul Bellow would appear in Rome, usually alone. He had, by the end, five wives, I think, and since they were all so alike I never put their names to memory. Each had a tendency to nag him for trivial lapses; "I told you *not* to forget the yogurt when you went into Red Hook," our common village. At one point he shared a house with Ralph Ellison between Edgewater where I lived and Bard College. I don't recall which of his wives was in residence while Ralph's brilliant wife lived in New York City and visited on weekends. Of contemporary American novelists only Saul was, properly speaking, an intellectual with a wide knowledge of philosophy and that small amount of history he felt connected to. It was always a relief to talk to him *about* many things as opposed to such dead-end subjects as academic tenure, best-sellerdom, and, inevitably, adultery, a major theme in the postwar novel. I was fascinated by Saul's *Herzog*, none of which, as far as I could tell, was invented, including the villainous Valentine based on one Jack Ludwig, a sort of primitive Iago never quite at home on the Hudson or in those groves of Academe where Mary McCarthy had also served time at Bard, giving rise to a brilliant satire of the world of Bard and what Terry Southern liked to call Quality Lit. The novel *Pictures from an Institution* was Randall Jarrell's response to Mary whom he calls Gertrude. "Although," he wrote, "Gertrude was not much of a novelist, she was a marvelous liar." What feuds there were in those days when *Partisan Review* ruled the roost and Delmore Schwartz was the great poet of the second Jewish generation! But Delmore's reign ended with the appearance of Robert Lowell who proved to be a far more brilliant careerist than the rest of the field despite occasional bouts of madness from which Delmore also suffered. In the end, Lowell was king of the castle while Delmore ended up as the protagonist in one of Saul's most generous novels, *Humboldt's Gift*. As I write these lines I find myself suddenly in the Gotham Book Mart, the bookstore that Frances Steloff had made a center of the "New York School" of the forties.

Life magazine did a famous photograph of twenty or thirty writers honoring Edith and Osbert Sitwell on their first tour of America. Although the N.Y. School did not think much of the Sitwells, Auden and Spender were also on hand. Auden, perched atop a ladder, picked a book off the shelf nearest him and handed it to me: *Problems of Men* by John Dewey. Riotously funny. Nearby, side by side, sit Jarrell and Schwartz. Tennessee and I are at the rear of this company. He had been amused when his old friend and fellow poet, Elizabeth Bishop, complimented him on a poem of his that she had just read in *Mademoiselle*. What else had he been doing? she asked. He mentioned *A Streetcar Named Desire*. Bishop simply smiled fondly and turned to Marianne Moore.

Sometime in the early sixties Saul came to me with a play he had written. I had already done two plays on Broadway so he wondered if . . . The play was called *The Upper Depths* and was not only funny but original; he had taken on the self-importance of entirely ordinary people who, thanks to the then current vogue for Freudian analysis, regarded themselves and their various tics not only seriously but solemnly

Saul Bellow, a Hudson Valley neighbor, also liked to
visit Rome where he paid us a call at our Largo
Argentina flat not far from a restaurant run by an
order of third-world nuns. Alberto Moravia occasionally joined us, to listen to their hymn-singing,
he declared.

because in the fraudulent would-be democracy of the postwar world *everyone*, by definition, was equally interesting and significant—and so if only enough attention were paid ... Saul for a time had been a Reichian and had even sampled that guru's orgone box. Joseph Anthony, who had directed my play *The Best Man*, agreed to direct *The Upper Depths*, a perfect title that metamorphosed into *The Last Analysis*, dealing with a TV comic far gone in megalomania as he conducts his own psychoanalysis on his own TV program. I still think the original script might work. But Saul never tried the theater again that I know of.

From time to time, even when Saul was well off from the success of his books, he would go back to teaching. When I asked why, he said: "Well, I know all sorts of people here in Chicago and I certainly like them better than that New York crowd but every now and then I want to talk about literature and so, when I do, I can call a class." Saul's dislike of New York where he had undergone coronation as the great novelist of his generation had been symbolically shadowed by a review of one of his later novels in *The New York Review of Books*: V. S. Pritchett's review was characteristically polite but unenthusiastic; worse, it was entitled "Alien Corn." Bellow never forgave the Epsteins who were among the founders of the *Review* or, indeed, the entire New York School that had raised him so high. He retreated to the "real" world of Chicago where he celebrated the likes of Allan Bloom and Leo Strauss in books like *Ravelstein*.

I seldom saw Saul in the last years. I think that the last time we saw each other was when he came to see me at our Rome flat in Largo Argentina. Since he liked Alberto Moravia (whose first name he always pronounced in three slowly deliberate syllables: Al-Bare-Toe), I took them to a restaurant run by a lay order of beautiful third-world nuns. I fear the two lecherous old masters ogled these psalm-singing nubilities. All in all, a cheery evening. At one point we spoke of death and what each expected to die of. Saul was very positive. "I expect to just wear out." And so he did, a man of Benthamite utility.

Biographies, memoirs, volumes of letters by friends and acquaintances keep arriving and are stacked in piles all around my workroom. Sometimes there are unwelcome surprises. Christopher Isherwood, a friend for forty years or so, wrote endless diaries, all reverently published word for word by his heirs. Since Chris seldom awakened without a horrendous hangover, the "hangover diaries," as I dubbed them, report his morning sickness, as it were, and give no sense of what the often joyous evenings before had been really like. With jaundiced gloom he took us all on. I had thought that between his native shrewdness and whatever Vedanta is supposed to do to heal or palliate the wounded psyche he might have written in a more generous vein. But he is often hard on those who had been good—and often more than helpful—friends like John Van Druten whose play *I Am a Camera* and subsequent musical, *Cabaret*, supported Christopher in his final decades. I come off fairly well. My political toughness was admired. But there is something claustrophobic about his total obsession with himself and domestic life. Little news from the outside world got through to him or, if it does, he promptly ignores it. The diaries to one side, he was still, in life, the consummate boy-charmer despite whatever age he had so unexpectedly found himself at. Of his new celebrity as a "Gay Icon" he reveled in the limelight. "Literally," he said. "When I'm out there on the stage with all the lights blazing away I am so relaxed—so at home—that I am in serious danger of falling asleep." The obituary style still clings, as it were, to my pen. After a successful prostate operation, he was told to check back, regularly, with the doctor, which he forgot to do. The cancer spread. Soon he was dwindling away. I had just come from London and paid him a visit. He was hardly present. I chattered nervously. Talked of mutual friends whom I had seen. Remarked upon the fecklessness of the British. After the bonanza of striking oil in the North Sea, the Thatcher government seemed to have gone through the money. I was censorious: "A nation of grasshoppers," I said. The old Isherwood, the Isherwood of legend, suddenly opened his eyes and smiled. "So what," he asked, "is wrong with grasshoppers?" Thus we parted, each in approximate character.

Although I answer letters from friends and even interesting requests for information, most of the fan mail goes into a large box which is eventually shipped off to the Houghton Library at Harvard. I've always kept just about everything that comes my way as did Lord Byron, Thomas Wolfe, and not many others, or so I've been told by university archivists. Fortunately, as a twentieth–twenty-first-century writer, ladies and page boys don't send me locks of hair as they did Byron. On the other hand, Vladimir Nabokov (whom I never met) and I liked to exchange elaborate insults through the press. In an interview he said that Graham Greene's conversion to Catholicism seemed entirely bogus to him while he had it, on the best authority, that I had gone over to Rome. These *épingles* as Vera Nabokov termed them ended when I remarked in an interview how odd it was that Russia's two greatest writers were of African descent. Before he could think of an answer, death ended these joyous exchanges.

Over the years, Louis Auchincloss and I exchanged a number of letters on many subjects from our common family to friends and, best of all, literary matters but where Saul could call a class I was obliged to write letters to only a few people like Louis Auchincloss, Paul Bowles, Isherwood, the Glorious Bird himself as I called Tennessee; we had a number of imaginary characters whose adventures cropped up in our correspondence. One was the mysterious Lesbia Ghoul, a ubiquitous figure forever on the move. April 5, 1948, Tennessee reports: "Lesbia passed through Rome, heavily veiled." (It was common knowledge that she had more than once submitted her tragic mask of a face to the surgeon's knife.) The Bird continues: "No sign of Willard. No word. Only a whisper of silk and a few rose leaves floating after. The scent of frangipangi. A few days later a gilt-edged card, saying 'Sorry' post-marked Istanbul, dictated, unsigned. With Lesbia one is never certain, such a thin line so easily crossed over! Nerves . . ."

There were numerous Lesbias and Willards in our peripatetic lives mostly around Europe and, thanks to Paul Bowles's urgings, Morocco which I disliked as much as the Bird did. But for the pleasure of Paul's company, each paid him calls, never together as it happened. Also, on the road, hunting in a pack, there were a number of remittance men, writers with no time to write, for which the Bird and I at least were grateful. Mostly Americans, they inclined to alcohol, kif, and to all the needy lads in the postwar poor countries. Since in those days I neither drank, nor smoked pot or kif, I had little in common with most of them. But Tennessee's love of the grotesque was positively Franciscan and he let them cadge money and not entirely empty bottles from the tourist hotels we stopped at if such places had, as he put it in that no-known language he sometimes used, *progresso libero*. In any case, spring and summer were for travel and constant work for each of us: he on his typewriter and I in longhand on yellow legal pads.

TWENTY

———————— ✳ ————————

In addition to plays and fiction (that season it was *Summer and Smoke* and several stories), Tennessee was busy writing letters which I am now, fifty-seven years later, reading for the first time in a New Directions volume. Tennessee was a wonderful letter writer tailoring his text to the recipient's likes and dislikes. In the spring of 1948 I was twenty-two and my third book, *The City and the Pillar*, was a bestseller. The remittance crowd was not friendly, to riot in understatement, nor were certain far-flung recipients of the Bird's letters. He was drawn to what I called monster women of which the most demanding and paranoid was Carson McCullers whose work I admired and often praised: the opening lines of *Reflections in a Golden Eye* reveal the American manner at its most perfectly focused. But she, alas, disliked me almost as much as she did Truman Capote whose *Other Voices, Other Rooms* was a greater success than anything Carson was to publish, but whose success she was convinced was entirely due to his unacknowledged borrowings from her work as well as from that of Eudora Welty. It was as if he, too, wanted to be a great Southern lady writer, and so raided their work for notions and pretty things. When Shelby Foote showed Eudora some of the passages from *Delta Wedding* that Truman had lifted for *Local Color*, she was serene. "Well," she said, "at least he took the things I liked best." Jane Bowles, another difficult serious lady, was also revered by the Bird. I only saw her husband, Paul, when she was otherwise engaged with her remittance men or her lady from the Tangier market who may have poisoned her, with datura leaves, bringing on a debilitating stroke.

One of Tennessee's earliest letters in this collection is to Carson McCullers. She was still seething over Capote. He introduces me warily. He and I had met at a party for Samuel Barber in the American Academy, I was staying at the Eden Hotel; he'd rented an apartment in the Via Aurora. ". . . Gore Vidal is here . . . Vidal is twenty-three [actually I was twenty-two] and a real beauty. His new book *The City and the Pillar* I have just read and while it is not a good book it is absorbing. There is not a really distinguished line in the book and yet a great deal of it has a curiously life-like quality. The end is trashy, alas, murder and suicide both." Thus he sets her mind at rest about the competition. Then, like a skilled matador, he lunges for the kill: "But you would like the boy as I do his eyes remind me of yours." With one shrewd thrust, starting with "beauty" and ending with the ultimate hemorrhage of life's blood on the subject of eyes, golden and otherwise, he ensured for me her lifelong loathing; yet I remained a public admirer of hers until the end though I do not love her better after death (to reprise a favorite poem of Tennessee's), nor did I feel too deeply the absence of her company over the ensuing years. In 2003 I attended a seminar at Yale to celebrate the fifty-fifth anniversary of the publication of *The City and the Pillar*, sometimes noted in academic circles as the basis for a new discipline called "Queer Studies." The "trashy ending" had been modified over the years to a fight and a rape. No murder, there was also never a suicide . . . I was in my youthful way trying to emulate Romeo and Juliet except that each lover was a boy. In other words, the ideal title should have been "The

Jane and Paul Bowles, having third and fourth thoughts.

Romantic Agony" but that title had already been used for a collection of essays by the Italian critic Mario Praz.

The Bird was a good critic but he seldom read novels if he could help it. Late in life he finally read *The Aspern Papers* and marveled at how close the story was to his own *Lord Byron's Love Letter*.

I think that what he once said of his own plays was also a factor in his reading: "I cannot write without a character for whom I do not feel sexual desire." Tennessee would occasionally give me stories he had written and I would do the same with him. Each was brutally frank with the other. I with his "Rubio y Morena," he as we have seen in the letter to Carson. Of the ending he had also told me, "I don't think you realized what a good book you had written."

After Tennessee died, Jay Laughlin his publisher at New Directions asked me to introduce a volume of his short stories, starting with, I think, a bit of juvenilia published in something like *Weird Tales* and ending with one of his last stories about an old writer racing literally from death as scraps of poems fall from his pockets. As I read the stories I realized that his talent and obsession was playwriting and the magical transference of text from written page to real actors who brought to life his true world both imagined and recalled. I also noticed the profound change in his work which mysteriously coincided with his change of name from Thomas Lanier Williams to Tennessee Williams. The style absolutely changes from . . . well, rather trashy naturalistic prose to that of a totally different voice quite unlike Thomas Lanier's.

I have just read a letter from the Bird to Oliver Evans, a poet-critic who thought, in his innocence, that Anaïs Nin was a great novelist. The Bird had just read *The Judgment of Paris*. With this seventh novel I had, without knowing it, much less planning it, found my voice: certainly, there was no dramatic change of name though publishing friends had assured me that the notoriety of *The City and the Pillar* would exclude me from serious attention and so perhaps I should pick a new name. I did: for three mystery novels that were glowingly reviewed in *The New York Times*. A decade later when I republished all three in a single volume over my own name, the *Times* attacked the three that they had so recently hailed as by someone else. But the Bird had, in his vague intuitive way, sensed something was happening when he read *Judgment*. On February 20, 1952, he wrote Evans who had complained about the book, "I am impressed by Gore's new book. I cannot quarrel with your analysis of it, but I am deeply impressed by the cogency of the writing and the liquid smooth style. And I think your article proves that you can do a piece on him. Give him my love. Say that the Bird gives her blessing." Thank God, poor Oliver left me alone. *The Judgment of Paris* and its successor *Messiah* has each had a long underground life, particularly *Messiah*. But by 1954 I had written my first play for television and Tennessee who had always thought me intended for dramatic writing was proved correct based on no evidence at all except his own peculiar intuitions. On January 30, 1950, he had written Laughlin that I had been in Key West and written "a really excellent story, the best thing he has ever done in my opinion"; "Three Stratagems" was published in the New Directions anthology 12 (1950) and also in a collection of stories called *A Thirsty Evil*. Tennessee then mentions an odd book that I think I had dictated as an experiment, the tale of a street hustler called *Some Desperate Adventure*. Since I have completely forgotten it I've sent away to Harvard for a copy. Tennessee is proving more and more on target as the years pile up between us. "It was the most honest expression of Vidal that he has yet offered. I am encouraging him to do it as a play. It could be terrifying as a study of the modern jungle. Vidal is not likable, at least not in any familiar way, but he and Bowles are the two most honest savages I have met. Of course Bowles is still the superior artist, but I wonder if any other living writer is going to keep at it as ferociously, unremittingly as Vidal?"

Well, thanks, Bird, from way up here in the awful year 2005.

TWENTY-ONE

————————— ✳ —————————

Over the years I suppose that I exchanged more letters with Tennessee's other honest savage, Paul Bowles, than ever I did with the Bird whose wisdom—now so terminally late in the game—I appreciate. For some reason Paul and I got into the habit of reversing names. He was Luap Selwob and I Erog La-div.

We first met in the forties in New York City when he was composing music for plays, among them *Streetcar*. Yes, in those days plays were literally *melo*-dramas; dramas with musical accompaniment somewhat on the order of the Warner Brothers movie music of the day which drove Bette Davis wild. During the shooting of *Dark Victory*, Geraldine Fitzgerald was on the set when Davis, having gallantly seen her husband off to New York and then planting a number of irises while going blind from some sort of fatal movie disease, makes her way, unsteadily, to the staircase. Out of view, the grips and everyone else nearby (was Ronald Reagan on hand? He plays a drunken playboy in the film; and is very good) gathered to watch Davis make her last climb up those stairs and to her stoic death.

Fitzgerald told me that "halfway up the stairs Bette stopped and turned to fix the director, Irving Rapper, with her famed steely gaze. 'Now tell me, Irving, before I waste any more time on acting, *who* is going up these stairs to die, me or Max Steiner?' " Like most of the great actresses she hated the schmaltzy movie music that was added later by some director-editor in order to nudge—shove—the audience into sobs or laughter. "What that awful music does," Davis said to me when she was playing in *The Catered Affair*, the first film that I ever wrote for MGM, "is erase the actor's performance, note by note," which was certainly true of Steiner's lush orchestrations but hardly true of the more evocative music that Bowles and Virgil Thomson and other "real" composers composed for the immediate postwar theater and films. But soon original theater music was dropped; union costs were too high for so precarious a medium where a single journalist on the warpath could shut down a production and often did, particularly in the case of the Bird and any other writer thought to be a same-sexualist. The fifties inaugurated an all-out war on the fags, which did much harm to the theater, an institution already besieged by movies and then swamped by television.

I have no clear memory of meeting Paul Bowles. Doubtless, it was when he was working on one of Tenn's plays. He was fifteen years older than I. A vivid blond with blue eyes. He had gone briefly to the University of Virginia; then fled to Paris to be a poet; was taken up—or was it taken in?—by Gertrude Stein and Alice B. Toklas. Bluntly, Gertrude told him he was not a poet. So he became a composer, and studied with Aaron Copland. He was a descendant of Samuel Bowles, the pro-Lincoln New England publisher (I was already investigating American history and told Paul more than he ever wanted to know about his interesting connection). Apolitical, he had briefly been a Communist as was the custom in those days in New York art circles. But he was deeply bored by the party and soon lost all interest in politics, unlike the Bird who awakened, after a decade's slumber, and said to me, "Gore, I think I slept through the sixties." I told him, "Bird, you didn't miss a thing but, if you were really asleep, God knows how you're going to deal with what's coming." But the Bird, undaunted, promptly joined the anti–Vietnam War movement.

Paul and Jane Bowles were both significant cultural heroes in that small New York world which honored the arts. Jane's witty stories and sardonic conversational asides were much quoted while his music with its Arabic themes became something of a cult. Lenny Bernstein, describing Paul's work to me, extended both hands: "After all these years I can still feel his music in my fingers. Perfect miniatures."

With some degree of guilt, Paul broke his marital pact with Jane and started to write stories and novels even more notable than hers. I can't say I was much aware of any of this at the time. I knew I preferred his company to hers—he was serene; she was often frantic. She made scenes over food in restaurants. When he bought or rented an island off the coast of Ceylon he asked me to join him. But I missed the boat by a day—he never believed my story. But it was indeed true. I ended up that winter at New Orleans in a Dauphine Street flat.

A recent biographer of Bowles quotes him as saying to me, "Why the hell didn't you write long ago and let me know that you had not taken the boat?" The lady biographer is inventing for Paul what she takes to be real American he-man dialogue that in no way resembles anything that he would have written, much less said to me. She also has another flight of fancy about Tangier and myself. As I have noted I went there twice in thirty or forty years only to see Paul not Jane. Now I read how, according to the lady, Jane is "caught up in a whirl of social activities being choreographed this time by Cecil Beaton, David Herbert, Gore Vidal, and Truman Capote." I had nothing to do, ever, with any of this cast of characters nor did I join in "whirls" of social activities for Jane or anyone else. My name has been idly inserted into a context where it doesn't belong. Then I read in her book that "biographer" Fred

Kaplan described Tangier in 1949 as "a gathering place for traveling queens attracted there by the weather, beaches, cheap cost of living, easy availability of drugs, and the Arab ethos that permitted every sort of sex under terms totally independent of European Puritanism. The town's dirt and widespread poverty, its total lack of intellectual culture, and the hovel Vidal rented in town, all were repugnant." This is the Kaplan style in high gear. But if Bowles's biographer invented this particular passage I find it actionable in court. I never rented—or set foot—in a hovel in Tangier. I stayed at the El Minzah hotel and never for more than a few days. If the lady biographer got this lurid nonsense from my "biographer" Fred Kaplan, who had been given a contract to complete the late Walter Clemons *authorized* biography of me, then Kaplan is the culprit. Later he claimed the book was not authorized and so he was boldly inaccurate as he let the chips fall where they didn't belong. He was interested in my sex life about which he knew nothing other than what little I had written in *Palimpsest*. I've not read his book other than an occasional passage—just enough for me to realize how accurate the headline of the review of his book in *The Times Literary Supplement* was: "On Misreading Gore Vidal."

Nonlinear lives make for awkward biographies by those who do not easily grasp the apparently conflicting identities—or masks—on view. When Paul came to write a memoir ("only for money" is how he always put it), he found himself as elusive to pin down as had these academic writers who tried to sum him up in conventional terms. Bill Burroughs had advised him to keep a journal but, always conscious of the *purpose* for writing anything, Paul could never determine for whom such a journal was ideally to be kept. If for himself it seemed idle, like making faces in the mirror. If for publication, like Gide, it seemed to him highly suspect, neither fish nor fowl.

Lately, while reading through Paul's selected letters, I found myself recalling more of him than ever before, since to each correspondent he showed a different face; he also liked the flat detail which often suggests more than what he appears to want to confide. In his novels and stories he has rendered so thoroughly his North African world, both real and dreamed, that one needs the letters to get some idea of his American world which never entirely ceased, particularly when he took teaching jobs in Florida and Southern California where he is like someone from another planet trying to separate the flora from the fauna.

I spent an evening with him in Santa Monica shortly before he was to teach his first class at San Fernando Valley State College of Northridge. Earlier offers to teach had fallen through because of his brief, perfunctory membership in the Communist Party. But, finally, he was vetted to teach at Northridge. "The only problem is," he said to me, "I have no idea what's required."

To Oliver Evans who taught at universities most of his life, Paul wrote rather desperately: "A Dr. Finestone wants to know what books I shall be using in my course. He also sent me my schedule: one meeting a week to consider creative writing (7pm to 10pm) and two a week to consider the existential novel (3 to 4:30) . . . Try to envisage my ignorance and explain to me what goes on in a classroom. What is a course? A lecture course? A seminar? A class? Who does the talking in each? What is the teaching process? Does one tell students one's own reactions to books?" I'm afraid this was pretty much his conversation with me at Santa Monica, only I knew less than he did about teaching. He had gone for a year, I think, to the University of Virginia while I had never set foot in a university except as an unconventional lecturer. In the end, he wisely taught his own books.

Paul had a difficult time with his memoir because he tended to remember places more than people. He had given his agent a list of famous people he had known and then discovered, a bit late, that he had little or nothing to say about them. In a letter to his publisher who had written that "the book seems to be more 'travel narrative' than 'subjective, personal commentary,' " Paul's answer was to the point: "If the mention of the people whom I have glimpsed on my way past them lacks precision in describing them, it is only because I never really *saw* them or thought about them, since for me they were manipulable objects to be used or somehow got around, in order to continue my trajectory . . . I'll do what I can to pad the passages on Williams, Vidal, Barnes, Guggenheim . . . and others." I now recall that at one point Paul asked me jokingly, I thought, if I could think of anything interesting or memorable that I had said or done when he was around. I replied, accurately, that I had forgotten me, too. Fiction writers with a gift for inventing other universes cannot be held to the journalist role of describing someone actually observed at large in quotidian reality.

But what Bowles does describe in his letters is a mounting horror of his native land. To the writer James Leo Herlihy, whose novel *Midnight Cowboy* Paul had liked, he writes:

What I admire beyond the style is the easy way [you] capture the United States and its particular essence, without, however expressing any opinion extrinsic to the story, without even a hint of disaffection. Wonderful! I suppose that strikes me because I've always been afraid to tackle America; I know quite well that my hatred would show through all defences. For years I've thought of a thousand points of view which would aid me in masking my feelings and thus make it possible to use the place as a locale for a book, but there seems to be no way. It may be you don't even have the murderous emotions about the US, but whether you do or don't the miracle remains. You've either hit on the right way of looking at it (from the beginning) or found a way of hiding your hatred. In the latter case, it would be literary skill; in the former, you could consider yourself blessed by fortune first of all. It doesn't matter either way.

But it continues to matter in Paul's next letter to Herlihy.

It still seems to me that the formalized life of primitives must be emotionally satisfying, if only because so many of the acts of daily life are performed in the manner of a ritual, and before witnesses. (Then I worry: Could it be that my nostalgia for that lost childhood

is merely a disinclination to assume the responsibilities that becoming civilized demands? Then I answer: No. We're still primitives. We don't really want to be civilized. In another ten *thousand*
years, perhaps.) . . . And about the hatred of America: naturally I
mask it, because I mask everything. Too much importance is given
the writer and not enough to his work. What difference does it
make who he is and what he feels, since he is merely a machine for
transmission of ideas? In reality he doesn't exist—he's a cipher, a
blank. A spy sent into life by the forces of death. His main objective
is to get the information across the border, back into death. Then
he can be given a mythical personality . . . I don't think a writer
ever participates in anything; his pretences at it are mimetic [Not
mine, Paul] . . . This all sounds far too serious. But you got me
started.

I rather wish that I had got him started rather than Herlihy. Both
Bowles and I had been influenced by Sartre's *La Nausée*. Writers of any
complexity are not well served in biographies by schoolteachers, particularly American ones. In 1989 Paul wrote the editor of Black Sparrow
Press how displeased he was with a recent biography of himself. He
quotes me as saying "that if I collaborated, half the material would
be wrong, and if I didn't, everything would be wrong. In the course
of events this was beautifully borne out." If only I had had me to advise
me (!) in a similar situation where everything was wrong.

I'm mildly surprised by Paul's intense dislike of our native land in
the year 1966. It is in part the fastidious dislike of a Flaubert for the
mindless cud-chewing of the middle class anywhere which can often
provide fuel in the form of spleen as well as satire in such private made-
up cities of the plain as my *Duluth*. But Paul seems uncommonly, un-
characteristically fierce in his declaration to Herlihy. But then I have
never thought the idea of a mere country could ever be sufficiently co-
herent to hate or to love as opposed to simply observe. I suspect that
Paul found unfathomable my interest in how the American experiment

was turning out—as exotic to him as I found his apparent passion for the primitive world of North Africa and other places to the far south and farther east. The idea of the writer as a Promethean figure crossing like a spy the boundaries separating life and death is a splendid metaphor for his own writing at its best, but the oddly bitter note he strikes with Herlihy he never did with me. I understand the disdain of high art for mediocrity but his objection is much deeper. He once defined decadence for, I think, *The New York Times* as "commercialism" and "a failure of energy," not their expected answer.

I've been putting my memory to work to find a vulgar root for his need to mask all things, including his dislike of his native land not too much different from that of our own American master Henry James.

Once, while Paul and I were waiting to cross Fifth Avenue, I started to go against the light. "Don't!" he said. Since there was no traffic, I asked him why not risk it? "Because my mother did when I was a child. She simply held up her hand and said, 'Nonsense, *we* have the right of way.' I stayed on the curb and she walked into the Fifth Avenue bus. She was lucky not to be killed." Paul never forgot that utterly mistaken concept: "*We* have the right of way."

Then there was his final break with the United States. He had entertained a youth at a hotel. The young man wanted money. Paul said no. The youth departed, to be replaced by two plainclothesmen. Since Paul did not have the cash they asked for, he made a date to see them the next day. By the time they returned, if they did, Paul was on the high seas. There are more details to the story but I have forgotten them. The essential point is that the criminalizing of drugs and sex is very much a sign of that malign primitivism which has always reigned in Freedom's Land. For Bowles, Morocco was freedom, particularly as he penetrated the high Atlas and the Sahara desert, recording music that he was certain could be traced back to Roman times, while noting down stories that go back to the early days of our race which gave us Puritan New England that also gave birth to that original mind, masked or not, of

Paul Bowles whose imagination responded with civilized hatred to the sort of primitive laws the two New York plainclothesmen were eager to exploit.

Despite my own troubles with my English publisher John Lehmann or, rather, his real and sometimes imagined troubles with British censorship, I got him to take Paul's *The Sheltering Sky* which had been rejected in the United States on the absurd ground that it was not a novel. Lehmann did well by the book and later with Paul's short stories. But Lehmann was too literary an English publisher to survive the deepening twilight of the Gutenberg age, in which only a few small American presses were thriving in the dusk. One was Black Swallow Press. In 1979, they wanted to collect in one volume Paul's stories. Paul wanted no introduction. But the publisher did. Paul was averse to the sort of academic who might latch on to such a project; then he said that he wanted me to do it . . . "Having respect for Vidal's critical mind I chose him rather than taking a chance on someone the publisher might find." I was delighted. There is nothing like having to do a critical piece not only to concentrate the mind on a subject as complex as Bowles but to work out what it is that most draws one to a given writer's work. With Tennessee's stories it was a tone of voice the like of which had not been heard since Mark Twain. Each was a comic genius within a dark universe that the innocent persist in calling home sweet home. Bowles proved to be something of an inhuman observer like one of those vividly colored parakeets he doted on. Or, perhaps, the spirit of one. I enjoyed all of the stories except a few at the end where he notes that he had written them on kif. I thought them not as compelling as "Pages from Cold Point" and "The Delicate Prey." He disagreed. Over the years he'd bring this up. After all, he'd say, everything he ever wrote had been written on kif, et cetera. He was also touchy about any hint that he had been influenced by the Marquis de Sade because he had found him boring; in fact, he said, he'd never really read him. I reminded him of that afternoon in Paris when he paid a lot of money to buy the Pléiade edition of Sade.

In due course Paul scrapped the collected edition and allowed his stories to fall back into their original small editions on the ground that a number of special volumes were more remunerative than a single large one.

Both Paul and Jane, together and separately, had, according to that polymath Virgil Thomson, dowsing rods for money. Libby Holman, the blues singer who may have killed her tobacco-heir husband, financed the Bowleses for years. It seems she had paid courtesy calls on Jane as well as developing a passion for Paul's Arab lover from Tangier. But, by and large, the principals in our curious world steered clear of each other. Paul told me that Jane had been the first to abandon their conjugal duties. She told others that he had given up first. Once in New York when Tennessee and I had been prowling together one summer night, without success, he said, "Well, I guess that just leaves the two of us." To which he claims I replied, "Don't be macabre." Donald Windham, his handsome collaborator on *You Touched Me*, when the Bird, in a similar situation, suggested that the two of them . . . Windham says he said, "I deplore your taste." Where the British—at least Bloomsbury—never ceased to have affairs with friends, colleagues, relatives, Americans of the same sort try to separate, wisely I think, sex and friendship.

Paul's last days were filled with various illnesses, the usual fate. But there was a successful concert of his music in New York. There were still twilight Gutenberg ceremonies where his crystalline prose shone as though darkness did not exist. There was a conversation with his biographer about the great influences on his life and career, and he mentioned Gertrude Stein, Aaron Copland (of course, he added), Gore Vidal, and Tennessee Williams. He died November 18, 1999, missing the first years of the twenty-first century and the last years of the American Republic, which his ancestor Samuel Bowles had cared so much about.

TWENTY-TWO

———————— ✳ ————————

I left myself at the end of my first memoir, *Palimpsest*, in the year 1964, when I was thirty-nine. It is now April 2005. I am in Los Angeles and at the beginning of May I shall have a cataract removed from my left eye. Everything they say about age proves to be true. For years I read to my blind grandfather and even led him onto the floor of the Senate. I also remember practicing being blind, eyes shut and walking, with arms outstretched. In World War Two, when we learned of the discovery of radar, my grandfather said, "Every blind man learns from personal experience about radar. As you walk toward a wall, say, you can feel the sound start to bounce off the wall, the principle on which radar is based." Although he was not given to self-pity he did complain how slow reading was for him, being unable to glance through a book and determine what, if anything, was worth reading in it. He also had his own special marginal symbols for important passages. If there was something he might want to quote in a speech he would say "Q," which one would write in the margin next to the passage to be remembered.

In old age he lacked the phenomenal aural memory of his youth when he used to bemuse the Senate with long lists of statistics that he had memorized, all the time holding a text in his hand which he pretended to read.

"I now grow forgetful," wrote Montaigne in old age. "Names refuse to come when bidden." It is encouraging to know that Montaigne who had read and reread everything worried about loss of memory, too. He was also fascinated by the process of memory: after all, he was the first great memoirist of life not only as lived by himself but as reported by others and written down.

"Off I go," Montaigne writes, "rummaging about in books for sayings which please me—not so as to store them up (for I have no storehouses) but so as to carry them back to the book, where they are no more mine than they were in their original place. We only know, I believe, what we know now: 'knowing' no more consists in what we once knew than in what we shall know in the future . . ."

It has been my experience that writers, myself included, often forget what they have written since the act of writing is simply a letting go of a piece of one's own mind, and so there is a kind of mental erasure as it finds its place on a page in order to leap to another consciousness like a mutant viral strain. I have just recorded Jane Bowles's uncharacteristic behavior as jealous wife only to recall that I had already quoted her letters to Paul in *Palimpsest*.

TWENTY-THREE

———————— ✳ ————————

I have now had a researcher prepare an outline of what I was writing and sometimes doing over the last forty years. Immediately after my return to the novel with *Julian*, somewhat perversely I took on a great deal of film work. One project was at the request of Ray Stark, a Hollywood producer, who found himself burdened with an unmakable screenplay of a best-selling book about the Nazi occupation of Paris. René Clément, a much admired French director—not least, as it proved, by himself and his formidable wife. He told me once that he had perfect taste. Howard and I holed up in a flat under the eaves of the Hotel Plaza-Athénée where Billy, our black spaniel, had distinguished himself by relieving himself on the carpet in the lobby as we were checking in. But the French tolerance of pets is their most distinguishing *amiable* characteristic.

The making of *Is Paris Burning?* was, as so often happens, far more interesting than the finished product. The previous writer, an American Francophile, had all the underground French freedom fighters constantly shouting *Vive la France!* He must have worked at Warner Brothers where films set in France were popular and the actors were either French or spoke their American English dialogue with heavy French accents. The fact that a script written in English to represent French speech could also contain many French phrases bothered no one. I would try to explain that the English spoken by the actors playing Frenchmen was, in context, French, and to clutter it up with numerous *zut alors* did not make the whole thing seem more French but simply confusing. My metaphysical arguments seldom won the day.

In Los Angeles Ray Stark had hired a young would-be filmmaker, a graduate of film school, Francis Ford Coppola, who could write an entire screenplay in a day or two. He was just what Ray had been looking for. Ray would give Francis a book like Carson's *Reflections in a Golden Eye*. Then, while Francis was working on the script, Ray would be persuading Elizabeth Taylor and Marlon Brando to play the leads. When they finally asked to see a script, Ray would give them Francis's handiwork with the explanation: "This is only a rough draft. Tennessee will be doing the final script." Ray was a great salesman and, of course, Tennessee never did do a final draft nor, sadly, did Francis. Ray was also not particularly grateful for how well Francis was serving him. As soon as I got to Paris, I sat down with Francis to go over my predecessor's script. There were a lot of "voilàs" and "Gallic shrugs" with strains of the *Marseillaise* on the soundtrack. I found Francis to be encyclopedic on anything that had to do with filmmaking. He was truly post-Gutenberg. Film was where *it*—all of it—was at. For him the written culture had passed into night, making him the first member of the total-film generation that I was ever to meet. Then I got a call from Ray: "Now that you're here I can let Francis go." I saw myself writing endless exterior shots: "*Long Shot*: German tank turns into Place de la Concorde—*Day*." I said, "No. I need him. He's done a lot of the exterior stuff already. I need him for that." On the personal side, Francis was in Paris with a young wife and baby. Reluctantly, Ray kept him on. Recently, Francis told me that I had turned him onto wine which, in turn, led to his becoming one of the leading winemakers in the United States. I asked him how I'd made this contribution. "Remember when we'd go out to lunch and you'd have a glass of wine and so would I though I didn't particularly like it at first? I associated wine with the older guys in the family who always drank red wine out of these Gallo jugs. I thought it was strictly for Italians hung up on the old country. Then you started talking about French wine and I was hooked." The reader who finds moviemaking interesting will note at this point that the director René Clément has not yet made an appearance. I'm sure he did in life but movies in those days were strictly controlled by the producer while the director, with a few exceptions, was simply a technician under the producer's guidance.

That season, Paris was particularly interesting for me due to the presence of Orson Welles who was acting-directing *Chimes at Midnight* at the Boulogne studio; he also played the part of the Swedish consul in *Is Paris Burning?*, a man who did his best to save a number of Jews from the Gestapo as Hitler's Third Reich was tumbling down. Hitler had determined that should his armies leave France, Paris must be burned to the ground. A good German and numerous brave and good French Gaullists and Communists prevented the burning. Orson was suitably cynical about our project but he was, as always, broke as well as deep into the role of Falstaff in *Chimes at Midnight*. After one lunch and six bottles of wine, we went back to the studio where Orson had been dubbing himself. On the screen was a picture of him, with lips moving. As he entered, he turned to a microphone and became Falstaff, not missing a beat. Considering what he ate and drank, it is amazing that he lived to be seventy. When he laughed, which was often, his face, starting at the lower lip, would turn scarlet while sweat formed on his brow like a sudden spring rain.

Orson was fascinated by politics. He had helped President Roosevelt with speeches. FDR thought him a born politician. But he was dissuaded from running for the Senate by "well-wishers" who said he could never make it because he was an actor and divorced. "Now look!" he boomed at his favorite Hollywood restaurant. "Look at Ronald Rea-

Orson Welles after lunch in *Is Paris Burning?* He was also moonlighting in the Bois de Boulogne acting in and directing *Chimes at Midnight.* Rudy Vallee, songster of yesteryear, kept sending each of us updates of his memoirs, which we used to study over lunch, particularly the trauma of the grapefruit someone hurled at him when he was onstage playing his horn; had it hit the horn, he keened, that golden voice would have been forever stilled.

gan! An actor and divorced!" Could an actor, I wondered, make a good president after a lifetime of being directed by others? Orson was ready for that one: "Suppose he'd been a director, too? But, even so, I'd trust Gregory Peck as president, if not as Captain Ahab."

Ray had a German co-producer whose task was to please, politically, the French Communist Party and the party of de Gaulle. Chaban-Delmas, a Gaullist politician, wanted to know who would play him. When told the beautiful Alain Delon, he was delighted. "Why, he looks exactly like me in the war." There were also a dozen or so American stars who played the victorious American army that arrived to secure Paris not quite ahead of the Free French troops who were incredibly bold to a man under Clément's rather nervous direction, nervous because of the political rivalries still going on. The German co-producer waited until Ray and I were gone. He then threw out most of our dialogue for the French characters and allowed the Gaullists and the Communists to supply their own dialogue, mostly great stunning clichés to demonstrate their overwhelming love of La France and la gloire. The result was purest chloroform. The picture ran for nearly three hours and at the gala American premiere the principal star in the audience was former vice president Richard Nixon, the only time I ever felt compassion for him. I had insisted that Francis get screen credit as a scriptwriter—his first. I then tried to get my name taken off the film but the lawyers worked too slowly and so my name remains. Later, when the film was shortened for television, some of it was not, visually, too bad. Vive la France! I also forced Ray to read a script that Francis had written. Gloomily, he read You're a Big Boy Now and then—gloomily?—he made it as a successful film, and so a great film career began.

Francis thought entirely in movie terms. To him, when we met on Is Paris Burning?, he was the young Budd Schulberg, while I was the washed-up golden-boy novelist of yesteryear, Scott Fitzgerald. The fact that several recent novels of mine were doing well went unnoticed. Twenty years later we met on a TV program. Francis was stout with a full white beard; he stared at me, bewildered. "Didn't you used to be older than me?" he asked. "That was just the movie version," I said. He gave me a bottle of wine from his vineyard.

After *Julian* 1964, *Washington, D.C.* 1967, *Myra Breckinridge* 1968, and on to now, I was once again a novelist-essayist-pamphleteer.

Washington, D.C. was the next to last novel, chronologically, in what publishers like to call my "American Chronicles," carefully avoiding my own title for the series, *Narratives of Empire*. I had been taken to task by *Time* magazine in a review of my first book of essays, *Rocking the Boat*. In order to show what a bad person I was, *Time* wrote that I had dared to refer to our minatory global presence as "an empire" which of course it could *not* be as we were, in the Luce publications, Christian goodness incarnate. It seems I had, once again, said the unsayable too soon. I was subversive.

But not entirely alone: today the only subversive programming on American television is C-SPAN. One would like to say it is because they try to take books seriously. But it is not book chat where C-SPAN is at its best; rather, for those of us fascinated by politics, congressional hearings as shown by C-SPAN in exquisitely boring detail are to me the only exciting and useful American television on offer. To watch senators and representatives fairly up close in Congress assembled affords us the only living look we will ever have of a government that is more and more secretive and remote not to mention repressive. Only the slowest among us—and I am one—are able to process yards of absolute boredom and feel revivified. Of course I was brought up in the District of Columbia when the Capitol was an almost lively place in my childhood. Also, D.C. was the domestic source of most secondhand news, as filtered through the print media. Now, with C-SPAN, we observe Senator Robert Byrd in eruption when faced with yet another usurpation of our liberties by an executive branch entirely geared for perpetual war and kept in office by one corrupted election after another bought and paid for by such masters of in-your-face corruption as Representative DeLay, who once dared We the People to try and bring him to justice, which he thought we could not do since he and his fellow operatives had control of the election machinery electronic as well as humanoid. Finally someone at C-SPAN had the bright idea of covering, from time to time, the British House of Commons at question time when the prime minister and his opponents are forced to answer questions of high policy, often impaling themselves on their own quibbling, though seldom on lies. This is democracy in action, something we have never actually experienced and may now never know.

Years ago the critic Dwight Macdonald noted that any letter to the *Times* of London (and Brits are addicted to substantive letter-writing) is sure to be better written than any editorial in *The New York Times*. At first hand, I can also attest that our own congressional voices fifty years ago were light-years superior to those today or to the halting subliterate style of our governing junta. Also, not only were the three recent British party heads (Blair, Howard, and Kennedy) more knowledgeable than their American counterparts, they were also quite able to deal with *a live BBC audience* whose average age seemed thirty or so while the twenty-somethings on hand were formidable, too. Blair got it not only from his rivals for the premiership but from a young man who wanted some action by government against bullying in schools. This is a real subject that Americans are taught to think of as character building for serial killers and inspirational for heavily armed children eager to thin their own ranks.

A young woman wondered why, under national health (utopian compared to our insurance/pharmaceutical anti-health services), it took forty-eight hours for a G.P. to grant her an appointment. Blair's unfamiliarity with this flaw in the health system got him booed by others with the same complaint. To compare their audience of informed average citizens—quaintly called subjects, thanks to the ubiquitous presence of the phantom crown—was jarring to anyone foolish enough to believe that the U.S. is at all democratic in anything except the furious imprisoning of the innocent, the joyous electing of the guilty.

TWENTY-FOUR

——————— ✳ ———————

It is sometimes harder to get out of local politics than into it. Some time after the 1960 election I was visited at Edgewater by Mike Prendergast who had succeeded Carmine di Sapio as head of New York City's Tammany Hall. Would I be the Democrat candidate for Senate? Since I was convinced that no Democrat could defeat Jack Javits, the Republican who usually voted like a Democrat, I said, no, thanks. But then Howard and I discussed the possibility of living in Rome, a city I'd fallen in love with as a schoolboy in 1939 and, again, in the fifties when I returned to write the script for *Ben-Hur*. Although Howard had many friends at nearby Bard College, he'd never really taken to the area, which was changing from agrarian to suburban thanks to IBM's plants in Poughkeepsie and Kingston. Our friend Alice Bouverie, one of the reasons that I'd bought Edgewater in 1950, was dead and Eleanor Roosevelt was dying. The last time I saw her she said, almost cheerfully, "There has always been something wrong with my blood; and they hope to do something about it at last." I wrote her a note, wondering if I should make the

Senate race. She wrote me a few lines; despite shaky handwriting, she was as practical as always. She was also not in the habit of advising others about their business. "People are what they are," she liked to say. She may have suspected that I was ready to follow Apollo's advice to Rilke and change my life which meant going to Rome and finishing *Julian* in the stacks of the American Academy's classical library on Janiculum Hill. During this time, Eleanor died of tuberculosis of the blood. I don't think she was ever fully aware, as a widow, how powerful she was, always ready to engage in dialogue except when Stalin, suspecting the president was murdered, insisted she have an autopsy performed. "Marshal Stalin doesn't know we are *not* like that," an ironic response in the light of later events. When Khrushchev came to the UN, she invited him to Hyde Park to view FDR's grave and talk politics. Khrushchev rushed from New York City to Hyde Park, saw the grave and rushed back. She was disappointed; also stoic. "Mr. Khrushchev," she told me, "is interested only in power and I have none." But of course she did, which *he* did not grasp.

I left New York on the Italian liner *Leonardo da Vinci* for what was to be a "celebrity cruise." A number of so-called celebrities would sail for free (to the annoyance, no doubt, of the paying customers). Paul Newman and Joanne Woodward saw me off. I was booked as far as the Piraeus where Howard would join me and we'd then move on to Rome and an apartment in the Via Giulia rented sight unseen. Howard had just recovered from an operation at Manhattan's Memorial hospital where a great lump on his thyroid had been removed. It was benign but in the anxious time it took to get him booked into Memorial I developed a duodenal ulcer.

Once the *Leonardo* was under way, feeling cut off from all the world, I drank a glass of milk for my ulcer and then went into the dining room to find Paul and Joanne seated at the captain's table. They had only pretended to see me off on the cruise when, actually, they too were fellow passengers on what we ungratefully dubbed the ship of fools. On the cruise Paul proved to be our star of stars. Women sometimes behaved oddly when they saw him. Once when we were walking down Madison Avenue, a large young woman came toward us from the opposite direction: quickly, he tucked his chin into his collar to hide those arctic blue eyes. He also increased his pace. "Keep moving," he whispered as we passed her. Then there was a crash behind us. "Don't look around," he said, looking around; then he broke into a run. "What happened?" I asked. "She's fainted," he said and leapt into a taxicab.

TWENTY-FIVE

— ✳ —

Although I have never enjoyed large parties, when Howard arrived in Rome we went to quite a few, largely to see the interiors of a number of palaces. Rudi and Consuelo Crespi were at the center of the city's social life which was like Rome itself—a bit on the sleepy side but the settings were splendid. Consuelo Crespi was a beautiful American with that very American urge to bring different sorts of people together. This works just about everywhere but not in Rome during the sixties. Everyone she asked to their flat in Palazzo Taverna gladly came but the various groups stayed together like floral arrangements, each rooted to its own Aubusson rug. One group would consist of the so-called black nobles, created by the Popes. Then the whites, ennobled by the kings. Literary figures like Moravia and Bassani stood apart in the corners, while movie people swarmed. A few years later I arrived at a Roman reception to find the current prime minister holding court. The hostess apologized: "They aren't making films at Cinecittà anymore so now all we get to see on television are politicians so everyone is starting to invite *them*. Odd, isn't it?" Although Consuelo and Rudi were most diplomatic there was no way that members of one group were going to commingle with members of another. By and large, the intellectuals who had a lot to say spoke no English while the aristos, thanks to childhood nannys, spoke perfect English but had little to say. So, one ended up learning a great deal about how to heat a five-hundred-room palace and nothing at all about *The Garden of the Finzi-Continis*. The only time I saw the Romans close ranks was against the Prince and Princess of Monaco. The Romans executed a sort of graceful military maneuver, leaving Rainier and Grace Kelly alone at the center of the room, radiating serenity. Since Grace and I had been under contract to MGM at the same time, I paid my respects. She was unchanged. We always talked about her uncle the playwright George Kelly whom we both admired; unfortunately, he was as right wing as Grace who, invariably, with flushed cheeks, would explain how FDR and the New Deal had stopped him from writing plays. I would slip quietly away. Across the room Howard was discussing the Oceanographic Museum at Monte Carlo, a subject dear to Prince Rainier who was interested in saving the Mediterranean over, to hear him tell it, the dead bodies of every Italian politician.

Grace and I chatted about distant romantic Hollywood, not that she pined for her days of glory. I did ask her once, why, at the peak of her career, she had quit to become, in effect, the doyenne of an amusement park. Her answer was to the point. "You know about the studio's makeup call?" I did. The actresses who were to work on any given day were staggered so that the makeup department would not be overcrowded as famous stars would be meticulously turned into reasonably accurate replicas of their best selves. "Well, my makeup call was still pretty late because I was still very young. But I have a tendency to put on weight. When I do, my call is earlier. On my last picture, it was . . ." she frowned at the thought of the dawn's early light which one day she would have to face as had Loretta Young and Joan Crawford and a host of stars of yesteryear some of whom were obliged to report to makeup before sunrise. "It was the sudden change in my makeup call that de-

The Princess of Monaco: having second thoughts about makeup call?

cided me it was time to go before I absolutely had to." There was no talk of romance, only the snuffing out of a career based upon the fading of her uncommon beauty. Nevertheless, there were those who were puzzled that after so much hard work to become the biggest movie star of her time Grace would quit to become Princess of Monaco. A worldly lady of my acquaintance purred the answer: "Never forget that she *is* from Philadelphia."

The last week or so in November 1963 Howard and I drove out to the beach at Ostia with Rudi and Consuelo. The beach was deserted but the day was perfect. We had lunch and swam and then drove back to Rome where Howard and I went to the theater that showed American movies undubbed. Midway through *David and Lisa*, an American actor named Jerome Courtland came up the aisle and said, "Kennedy's been shot." This is not possible was my first reaction. Someone had mixed up the reels and we'd been given the wrong ending. The first of several as I shall note in due course.

Our first Roman years, in the Via Giulia and later on the Largo Argentina, movie production was at its peak and, for a few years, many movies were made at Cinecittà the principal Roman studio. During the late fifties I had worked on the script of *Ben-Hur* in an office next to that of the producer Sam Zimbalist. Farther down the corridor from my office, Federico Fellini was preparing what would become *La Dolce Vita*. He was fascinated by our huge Hollywood production. Several times we had lunch together in the commissary. Soon he was calling me Gorino and I was calling him Fred. Neither Willy Wyler nor Sam wanted to meet him because both were aware of a bad Italian habit which was to take over the expensive sets of a completed American film and then use them to make a new film. I think that this had happened with *Quo Vadis*. To prevent the theft of *Ben-Hur*'s sets, guards were prowling the back lot long after production had been shut down. But before that, I had sneaked Fred onto the set of first-century Jerusalem. He was ecstatic.

Over the years we saw each other, from time to time; usually, when he wanted something. Fred disliked scripts even though his best film, *8½*, was written by Italy's finest playwright-essayist Flaiano. When they eventually fell out, Fred simply stopped telling stories for the screen. He also disliked professional actors so when he had to people a set he would call on an endless supply of headwaiters and cooks from his favorite restaurants to "act" in his films. Since there was seldom a script he would ask his cast to count on camera. Finally, when he got the look he wanted, he'd say "Twenty-eight" to the "actor." "Do twenty-eight again." The results were often surprisingly successful, yet he complained about his films' lack of success at the box office. I said his refusal to film with direct sound was certainly a factor. As with so many Italian directors of the first postwar generation, his actors were shot as in a silent movie; then a voice, seldom their own, was later dubbed in. "Why are you people so crazy about direct sound?" he'd ask when once again a request for money from a studio was rejected because he would not swear an oath to make the film with a script in English that would be approved and then used. I tried to explain that all the great stars of the thirties and forties whom he admired were famous for their voices but Fred had never heard those voices because most of the American films that he had admired in youth had been dubbed into Italian.

He rang me one day. "We must meet immediately." He came to Largo Argentina, all smiles of a guileless childlike nature. "Gorino is problem."

"*Casanova*?" I made a guess.

"How you know?" Eyes wide with alarm as if I were a master of dark arts. Of course his inability to finance a film about Casanova had been for some time on the front pages of the Italian press. I gazed thoughtfully into an imaginary crystal ball. "Yes," he said, "is *Casanova*. I need one million dollars to begin. Paramount will give it on condition—"

"That you shoot in direct sound from a script in English."

He nearly made the sign to ward off the evil eye. "*You* know *all* this?" Eyes narrowed at my superior cunning. "Ah, of course *they* tell you, don't they?" I assured him I was simply psychic. He looked relieved.

We talked about the story. His Casanova would not be the brilliant man known to history, the friend of Voltaire. "No, the real Casanova is silly. Is always sex with him." Fred's sex life was a much discussed enigma in Rome. He was happily married to the actress Giulietta Masina. Fred's passion, at least visually, for huge-breasted women was known to everyone who ever saw one of his films but what did he *do*? I suspected nothing. During the days of lead when the Red Brigades were loose in Rome he feared being kidnapped. "I am too large," he'd say, close to tears, "to fit into the boot of a car."

Once, I mildly complained that he had borrowed from my novel *The Judgment of Paris* the character of a hermaphrodite who is the center of a religious cult. No, he'd not, of course, read the book but Eugene Walter, an American writer in Rome, had and a version of my character appears in *Satyricon* which Walter worked on. Fred denied any need to borrow such a character. "Why should I? When I . . . I am a hermaphrodite! Is well known, Gorino." Then he gave me a short treatment of the scenes he wanted for *Casanova*. "I know you will hurry," he said. I hurried. The script was accepted by Paramount. He got his million, a start date, and a star, Donald Sutherland, an intelligent actor. But a newspaper photo of Sutherland arriving in Rome to play Casanova suggested that there might be a difference of opinion between star and director. As if by magic, Fred appeared in Largo Argentina. He looked worried. He asked me if I knew Sutherland. "Yes, he'd acted in a play of mine for the BBC."

"I am thinking about getting Mastroianni."

"What's wrong with Sutherland?"

"He doesn't *look* right." This was fatal. When Fred was casting he'd have a couple of dozen photographs of possible characters and he'd stare at them by the hour until he found the one he wanted. Appearance was all.

I couldn't figure out why Sutherland, whose appearance Fred knew in advance from films, had not measured up.

"You know Casanova. *You* write Casanova," he began to shift blame. "Is very stupid man. No?"

"Actors can usually play stupidity . . ." I was reassuring.

"Must *look* stupid. See? I have made silhouette of him." Fred was a fine caricaturist. He showed me a drawing in black ink of Sutherland. "See? He looks just like prick." ·

I said I recognized the likeness. Fred looked again at his drawing, already feeling better. "I want to make empty place between two front teeth. Looks more stupid, no?"

I had now grasped, as it were, the point to Fred's image of the world's most famous lover as nothing but a blind soulless erection. I thought of the newspaper photo of Sutherland in a broad-brimmed hat and a flowing cloak, the spirit of romance: they were at odds. "You think he has caps on front teeth?"

"How would I know? Many actors do." I tried to imagine Fred with his drill hacking away at poor Sutherland's teeth. Although Fred was hardly a hermaphrodite he was certainly a phallophobe in a culture rooted in phallophilia. He had even done a book of caricatures of phalluses, with such labels as "the happy cock," "the snobbish cock," "the angry cock." He entertained ladies with these drawings.

Fred vanished. The film was eventually made not in direct sound but dubbed. Fred was entering his final phase which produced only one fine film, *Amarcord*, reminiscent of his great phase in which I had once worked for him as an actor.

Since I have always wanted to know how interesting things actually work, I had signed a contract as a writer for MGM because I knew that the great studios were going to break up—this was in the mid-fifties— and I was curious to see what it was like to work at the greatest studio of them all: Metro-Goldwyn-Mayer.

It was amazing to realize that everything necessary to the making of a film was right there on the so-called lot at Culver City, including the Thalberg Building where, on the top floor, L. B. Mayer had his office and access to an executive dining room. The powerful producers had their offices at the corners of each of several floors below; while smaller offices, containing writers, were placed alongside their masters, the producers.

From the beginning I worked with Sam Zimbalist who had made a number of successful films, often with Clark Gable and the director Victor Fleming who was to replace George Cukor, at Clark Gable's request, on *Gone with the Wind*. According to Cukor the young Gable had been a male hustler and George was one of his johns. In Actors Studio circles, where I had spent much time, it was agreed that Gable must have been more of a Stanislavski actor than anyone had suspected if he felt that Cukor's presence on the set might undo his impersonation of Rhett Butler. My mother had had a long off-and-on affair with Gable going back to the film *Test Pilot* where the flying was done by what would eventually be her third and final husband the Army Air Corps general Robert Olds who was then aide to the chief of the Army Air Corps Billy Mitchell. Gable was an amiable man who often visited my mother at the Beverly Hills Hotel where I was an occasional visitor during my convalescence from hypothermia at Birmingham General Hospital. Gable even taught my very young half brother, Tommy, how to swim in the hotel pool; he was a most professional teacher but the lessons ended when Tommy, clinging to Gable's back and imitating his arm gestures, relieved himself comfortably on his back. That was the end.

At MGM I wrote *The Catered Affair* for Sam as well as *I Accuse!* about the Dreyfus case directed by José Ferrer who also played Dreyfus. Halfway through the editing Eddie Mannix, speaking for the front office, asked Ferrer to cut any references to Jews. This was not easy to do in a film about anti-Semitism. Finally, the picture was not too bad but it is still mysteriously banned in France. When MGM bought the Elstree Studios in London I wrote *The Scapegoat* starring Alec Guinness and directed by the brilliant Robert Hamer who had written and directed *Kind Hearts and Coronets*. Unfortunately Robert had also taken seriously to drink; otherwise I would have withdrawn and fought for him to write as well as direct the script, a Daphne Du Maurier romance. By then my curiosity about the studio system had waned as had the studios themselves. But I was still curious about film acting.

When I was on leave from the army hospital, I was offered a screen test at RKO to play one of Rosalind Russell's sons. Since I was writing my first novel in the hospital, I said no. But for someone brought up in the Golden Age of movies I sometimes wondered what if . . . ?

TWENTY-SIX

——————— ✳ ———————

Suddenly, there was Fred. "I make film about Roma. I want you and Sordi and Magnani and Mastroianni." I asked *why*? This was Fred's least favorite word. He was a droll and inventive liar and his verbal arabesques were for the most part entirely wasted on flatfooted showbiz interviewers. He blinked his eyes as if in thought: *Why?* We were in the restaurant of the Grand Hotel where he would establish himself at a special table set in what looked to be an opera box. "Because," he said, "you all live in Rome and you are all from outside." I laughed: "Magnani is Rome." He realized his mistake. He waved his hands. "She is from everywhere. Like the sun. The moon. The . . . I have one question I will ask each of you who can live *any*where: Why you live in Roma?"

My scene was shot in a small square off Via dei Coronari . . . It was a freezing February night but we were all dressed in summer clothes, pretending it was the August Trastevere festival of *Noi Antri*. Tables and benches were scattered around the square. Huge plastic fish were on display in tubs. Howard and I sat at a table with three or four American

It is 1973 and I am playing myself in *Fellini's Roma*. Between takes Fred, as I called him (he called me Gorino), would sit beside me at an outdoor table on a freezing cold Roman night, which we were pretending was a hot evening in August during the Trastevere festival of *Noi Antri*. I wear light August clothes; Fred is bundled up in overcoat and hat, with a heater just back of his chair. I shivered through the scene, actually shot in the Via dei Coronari.

friends. I was fascinated to find that Fred worked much the way Picasso did in the documentary where he paints on a sheet of glass while the camera shoots from under the table so that we can see what he is painting, as he erases, transforms, restructures. Plates of food kept arriving. Wine bottles. More plastic fish. Some tourists sit at a table opposite us. Fred directed his cameraman as he kept filling in the background with people, food, decorations. When *Fellini's Roma* was released in 1972 (Fred's name was part of the title), he was also ready by then to tell the world why he had picked his four stars. "I pick Mastroianni because he is so lazy, so typical. Alberto Sordi because he is so cruel." An odd characterization: Sordi was a superb comic actor whom one did not associate with cruelty but then, at the core of comedy, there is indeed a level of sharp observation that the ones observed might easily regard as cruel. "I chose Anna Magnani because she is Anna and this is Roma. Vidal because he is typical of a certain Anglo who comes to Roma and goes native." As I never spoke Italian properly, much less Roman dialect, and my days were spent in a library researching the fourth century AD, I was about as little "gone native" as it was possible to be but Fred clung to his first images of people. He wanted us all to improvise our dialogue on why we were living in Rome. I like improvising and since Fred never listened, particularly to English, that part was easy. I said something about a world dying of overpopulation and the poisoning of the environment, two new concepts for most Italians that year (one journalist even wrote how ridiculous I was to speak of these matters when he had never seen so much food in the shops). Then Fred and I had a row. I insisted on dubbing my own voice in English, French, and Italian (yes, there was, yet again, no direct sound). Fred was hurt. "Gorino, you no trust me?" I said, no, I did not: he was quite capable of inventing *anything* he wanted for me to say in three languages and I'd be duly quoted forever. Finally, he agreed. As I went into a fourth or fifth version of a speech that ended with "What better place to observe the end of the world than in a city that calls itself eternal?," at that moment what sounded like an atomic bomb went off behind me. I turned to see four magnificent white horses drawing a large wooden wagon. The clatter of their hooves filled the square. Like Picasso, Fred had found his background a bit empty; hence, the horses and the wagon.

It was a long night. In the end I survived and the horses ended on the cutting-room floor. Some months later I was summoned to a studio to dub my voice. On a large screen there was my scene. Fred looked contented. Since he had lost the soundtrack of the original scene, nothing but odd noises could be heard on the screen. I asked, "Don't you have a transcript of what was said?" Fred winked. "No, Gorino. We just make up something else." For two hours I sat trying to match words to my own lips on the screen. Fred was quietly triumphant at this victory in his war against direct sound. Finally I cobbled together three sets of words in English, French, and Italian. Then we started to record. There was a white ball that bounced along the top of the screen and when it stopped you stopped speaking, your dialogue presumably in place. I got through the French and the English easily, but Italian is longer than English and after the ball had stopped I was still speaking—*outside* the scene. Fred was gazing beatifically out the window as I struggled to keep up with the ball. After the third ruined take, I said, "You are considered the greatest living film director, so give me some direction. How do I end this speech with the bouncing ball?"

"Oh, *is* there trouble?" His eyes were wide with innocent concern. "Oh, is so *easy*. Before you talk, you take deep breath." I did and the shot was perfect, concluding my career as a screen actor in Italy.

A researcher notes that I began writing *Myra Breckinridge* in June 1965. I didn't remember the date but I recall the day vividly. Howard and I had pretty much finished fixing up our Rome flat. I had a pile of lined yellow legal pads on my writing table which was opposite my bed. Across from the table a French door opened onto the terrace that overlooked the Largo Argentina—a great square with several Roman temples beneath the pavement's level as well as a large colony of cats that flourished until the Rome city government complained that they were sick and spreading disease. The fact that they spread diseases that only

The logo of the novel *Myra Breckinridge* was a giant statue of a Las Vegas showgirl, which twirled in front of the Chateau Marmont hotel on Sunset Boulevard. Jim Moran, a publicist who once hid a needle in a haystack, drove the statue across America presenting it to a dozen governors who each saw fit not to accept.

they were subject to cut no ice with the city fathers and so, to the rage of a number of old Roman ladies who regularly fed the cats, they would be carted away. I did state, publicly, that as the cat was sacred to the goddess Isis whose temple had been here, to harm them was sacrilege. Of course, in time another cat generation settled into the ruins. Meanwhile, the grateful Isis smiled upon me. The day I started *Myra Breckinridge* there was a new silver moon just risen over the Vatican to the west of the apartment, a sign for me of good luck; the moon not the Vatican. Curiously, when I finished the first longhand draft, there was again a new moon. One month had passed. Also, as I was writing just now about the cats of Isis, I got a call from Italy that our thirteen-year-old cat has just died of a liver problem; only his tortoiseshell kid brother survives of all those dogs and cats that for half a century accompanied Howard and me down the years. R.I.P.

Although when I set a novel in history I do a great deal of note-taking from the necessary records, when I start an entirely invented book like *Myra* I seldom start with anything more than a sentence that has taken possession of me. In this case "I am Myra Breckinridge whom no man may possess; clad only in garter belt and one dress shield . . ." The voice roared on. Who was she? I could only find out if I kept on writing. She was obsessed by Hollywood movies. That was soon clear. No matter how kitsch a film she could swiftly penetrate its mystical magical marshmallow core. Even so, it was not until I was halfway through the story that I realized she had been a male film critic who had changed his sex; Myron had become Myra. Why? I wrote on, laughing.

TWENTY-SEVEN

———— * ————

Politics now interrupts my return in memory to that happy time in Rome. So I must leave *Myra Breckinridge*, all aroar on her lined yellow pages, while I ponder the film that I saw last night; *The Deal* stars David Morrissey as the real-life British labor politician Gordon Brown, currently chancellor of the exchequer. The deal is the one allegedly made between him and Tony Blair—two ambitious young politicians—before the election of 1997 that would make one of them prime minister with the understanding that after one or two terms he would step aside and let the other take his place. Though British journalists discuss "the deal" as though they themselves had been witnesses to it, the film looks to be accurate, unlike most American attempts at political dramas of this sort. In the matter of the deal itself, the film shows the studied ambivalence of Tony Blair as he sets forth from Glamis, armed only with a toothy rictus smile and bright vulpine stare; in a telling scene with Brown, he does not quite admit that there ever was such an agreement other than he had felt that Brown was their party's *natural* leader: unfortunately, too many others preferred Blair's easy managerial style to Brown's old-fashioned seriousness, so he had no choice . . . At the time of the late election which won Labour a third term, a unique event in that party's history, Brown was not only the party's favorite but was also admired for the contribution his chancellorship had made to the United Kingdom's economic prosperity; while the prime minister, thanks to his passion for the Bushite illegal wars against Iraq and Afghanistan, had appalled many Britons who thought Blair should have stepped aside for the less tarnished Brown; also, Blair was generally believed to have lied to the nation when he maintained that his own attorney general had assured him that his decision to join Bush in the preemptive war on Iraq was legally sound when it was plainly not, according to the attorney general's actual memo as finally revealed.

Back in 1997 when the BBC invited me to the United Kingdom to cover the election, I went, first, to each party's initial announcement that it would fight the coming election for control of the House of Commons. The Labour Party met in a handsome eighteenth-century hall. TV cameras were everywhere; print journalists, too. We were led into a sort of back room where on a low dais, faced by rows of folding chairs, sat Tony Blair and his Shadow Cabinet. I sat at the center of the first row a yard away from the Shadow Home Secretary David Blunkett, a blind man with a large black seeing-eye dog. The dog and I made immediate eye contact. The dog was an old hand at political meetings. He was also bored, chin resting on outstretched front paws; he gave me a friendly yawn. I yawned back. He shut his eyes. Almost directly across from me was Blair, looking smaller than life. According to the press his handlers had ordered him to ration his tic-like smile. So, solemnly, tight-lipped, he stared, one by one, at the TV cameras all around the room. But, apparently, my yawn to the dog had set off a Pavlovian response in Blair who managed three yawns in a row with mouth firmly shut, forcing air uncomfortably through his nose and suggesting to me that he has a deviated septum. Back of him, to his right, was Gordon Brown darkly morose as he endured the first phase of the deal: the party leadership of Tony Blair and Labour's almost certain majority in the next Parliament followed, presumably, by the premiership of the other dealer.

As I recall, Blair took questions from the journalists, who raised their hands; I raised mine, too, but he only took questions from parliamentary journalists whom he already knew. The questions were perhaps more interesting to a foreigner than the answers which were intricately banal. Yet when a mildly sharp question was asked, the ghost of the rictus smile, like a negative undergoing slow exposure, would appear and Blair would say, gently, "Trust me!" That was that. But interesting, even dramatic changes were being made that day. If I had inquired more deeply, I might have unearthed the deal; in itself of no particular interest except to the dealers; yet, politically, Blair versus Brown represented the end of the old class-based party and the rise of a new managerial apparatus that represents administrative numbers rather than any specific class interest.

After Blair and Labour won in 1997, the journalist-politician Roy Hattersley wrote that Blair had "taken the politics out of politics": he'd made *New* Labour out of Labour. Once elected, Blair called in Hattersley for a chat. Blair was sunny. "I didn't, as you wrote, take the politics out of politics, but I was one of the first to notice that politics had already been taken out of politics." Why? Because a majority of the voters now believe that they are middle class. Since this is demonstrably untrue (today many "poor" Americans think of themselves as in the top percentiles of income), Blair's analysis is as applicable to the United States as it is to the United Kingdom. Particularly when he made the point that in political systems like ours you cannot have a real political party without a class base. Old Labour was real; it was made up of real working people. While FDR's Democratic Party coalition lasted triumphantly until his heir Lyndon Johnson did the one saintly thing of his checkered political career and intoned: "We shall overcome," knowing, as he said to friends at the time, that by enfranchising African American voters he had lost the *white* Southern vote to the Republican

Party—perhaps for all time. FDR's party of northern city machines plus organized labor plus repressed African Americans in the South was unbeatable for decades until Johnson—well, no good deed, et cetera.

The U.K. has no bloc of potential power quite like the African subjects of the old Confederacy. Even so, neither the Democrats nor the Republicans can now claim a class basis for their incoherent factions, only a possible collision between Bush imperialists and Dean anti-imperialists. So, as things fall apart, only the center appears to hold . . . barely. Good luck, Britannia. Good luck, Uncle Sam.

TWENTY-EIGHT

———————— ✳ ————————

I first knew Rome in 1939, a city where peasants, reeking of garlic, came to market rather like their counterparts (less the garlic) in Washington, D.C., while Mussolini's Blackshirts were everywhere. Then there was the Rome of 1948–1949 inhabited by Tennessee and Frederick Prokosch, a poet-novelist, while such composers as Gian Carlo Menotti and Samuel Barber were to be found at the American Academy. Life was still wartime austere but the dollar exchange rate was all in our favor which made life easy for us if not the Romans. Tennessee took a ground-floor flat in the Via Aurora a block or two from Via Veneto and the gardens of the Villa Borghese. I stayed nearby in the Hotel Eden, living off the fortune I'd earned from *The City and the Pillar*, a vast $20,000. Although I was supposed to have gone to Harvard after I got out of the army in 1946, joining many of my Exeter classmates, I had decided that after a lifetime of being institutionalized (imprisoned is more like it) in a half-dozen boarding schools, summer camps, the awful Los Alamos Ranch School where each boy had his own horse (mine was an ambulatory boneyard aptly called Two-bits)—the Ranch School was seized by the army and became the birthplace of the atomic bomb—then after nearly three years in the army, the thought of four years at Harvard was unbearable. Former Exeter classmates thought I was plainly doomed (I had no trust fund). I would "live by writing," I said. And so I did to their amazement—even chagrin since many of them had literary ambitions but some of the most talented had lost their nerve in the war. Though "nerve" is hardly the word. "Will" is possibly better. A friend at school, Bob Bingham, was energetically ambitious prewar, but when the war ended and he tried his hand at novel-writing somehow he was out of focus. He had had a bad time of it in the infantry in France where Lewis Sibley, another classmate, was killed: Sibley was already a distinguished poet at seventeen. A year ago I read some of his poems over WBAI radio in New York. The response was as wonderful as it was sad. The infamous "Battle of the Bulge" in France during winter must have been a particular horror for barely trained eighteen-year-old soldiers. Later, I was shown some of Sibley's letters. The army with its unerring gift for placing people where they would be least useful and most vulnerable had made the nearly blind Sibley a scout. His reported adventures began when his only pair of glasses was broken and the army's difficulty in supplying him with a new pair reduced his utility as a scout in freezing weather. That he should not, near-blind as he was, have been placed in the infantry was a sign of the general madness of that Good War as it lurched toward a victorious conclusion thanks to Soviet ground troops. Eisenhower, for political reasons, had held back General Patton's army so that the British Montgomery could at least look competent and the Russians could get to Berlin first, all of which did nothing much for American morale. Anyway, Sibley, wearing new glasses, was duly massacred just as another schoolmate—from St. Albans, not Exeter—was being embraced in a foxhole on Iwo Jima by a Japanese with grenades on his belt that democratically blew out both their stomachs. It is my impression that the so-called "best and brightest" were routinely killed off which might explain the notoriously low level of those now in political life and, to be fair, in the arts as well. Recently, I looked through the 1943 yearbook of our graduating class. As I looked at the pictures, trying to figure out who was who, I was struck by how old we all looked. For the most part, our graduating class averaged seventeen years old; yet there was a photo of three seniors standing side by side; they look as if they are in their early forties. Of course within months of graduation we would all be in the war and so it is possible that kindly fate was telescoping for us the selves that we might have become. Since a number of us would soon be dead, we were being allowed by a jocular nature—or by a magic Kodak—to see ourselves not only grown up but middle aged as well. There is a picture of Bingham and me on a lawn in back of Langdell Hall where I roomed. I am lying on the grass with a book, he is standing over me. We were both editors of the *Exeter Review*, the school's literary magazine which gave rise, under Bingham's managing editorship, to more intricate rows than any I was ever to encounter, grown up, on the board of *Partisan Review*. In a way it was nice of fate to give us all a preview of what we were not apt to live long enough to experience for real. Bingham ended up as an editor at Max Ascoli's *The Reporter* and, later, as a sort of managing editor at *The New Yorker*. We saw little of each other, once grown. Then, one day I got a letter from him to announce that he had a brain tumor and it looked as if he was going to precede me into the long night. Bob and his wife came to Rome but I was away and Howard took them out to dinner. I asked Howard for details. "Well, it was like they had made themselves up to look older, with gray hair and all that." Rather the way the 1943 yearbook had added a dozen or more years to those of us perhaps most vulnerable to an early death and so presumably curious to get a preview of what we might have become.

I recall in grade school that often a class would vow that in twenty years we would all meet again to see what time had done. But at Exeter, even without the devouring war in wait to pounce, we had no time for such sentimentality. Although most of my relationships with classmates were fairly amiable, once the war was done, I saw Bingham only a few

Bob Bingham is standing; I am on the grass—outside Langdell Hall where I lived at Exeter. We are about to quarrel over which stories were to appear in the next issue of the *Exeter Review* which we co-edited much of the time, a nice preparation for later serving on the board of *Partisan Review*.

times over the years with another classmate, A. K. Lewis, who had worked with me in the summer of 1942 at a Camden, New Jersey, factory where molded plywood wing tips for fighter planes were made. I was hopeless at the work; he was not. Years later he wrote the script for a wonderful movie called *Klute*. At Exeter we had made a schoolboy bet about which one of us would lose his hair first. Thirty years later, in Hollywood, he paid me the $100 that he owed me and I spent it on our dinner.

I have not gone to any of our class reunions. I can't think why.

Back to Rome in the sixties. Like Venus, Myra Breckinridge rose or rather leapt from her sea of yellow legal pads. Meanwhile, Roman life agreed with both Howard and me. All sorts of people that we knew and did not know came through town: memorable was Isherwood on his way back from a first visit to India whose Vedanta texts he had written so much about. Overwhelmed by the subcontinent's proverbial teeming millions, he foresaw, with some equanimity, the eventual dying out of the fragile white race. "But we must," he said solemnly, "set aside reservations for the better-looking blonds, the Danes and so on. They must be preserved like rare unicorns. Certainly, the Indians will enjoy them in their reservations along with all that snow we'll shovel in to provide the right Arctic touch."

I gave the completed *Myra* to my editor Ned Bradford at Little, Brown—a Boston publishing house. I hoped that Ned and the publisher, Arthur Thornhill, would not be too upset by Myra's exuberant pansexuality. Fortunately, they were not.

TWENTY-NINE

————— ✳ —————

My very first publisher, E. P. Dutton, was run by a White Russian called Nick Wreden. When I was still in uniform, he had taken *Williwaw*, my novel about an army ship in the Aleutian Islands during the war. An ursine figure of jovial disposition, during the days of my blackout by *The New York Times* Wreden loyally kept on publishing me. While I was busy writing plays for television, movies, theater, Wreden had moved on to Little, Brown and despite several published obituaries of me as a novelist (apparently, once lost to television that was indeed the end of someone who'd been thought promising), I told Nick that when I got back to novel-writing I'd come to him. But when, like General MacArthur, I did return, Nick was dead, and his place at Little, Brown had been taken by Ned Bradford. I have never needed an editor in the sense of a Max Perkins who was so necessary, we are assured, to salvage the likes of Thomas Wolfe, by neatly shaping long flowing works into simple commercial slices. All I ever needed was an intelligent first reader and, later, a good copy editor. Bradford proved to be ideal. When he read the manuscript of *Julian* his only comment was embarrassingly to the point: "You forgot to tell us *why* he became a Christian apostate." I promptly provided the missing link. The three novels that I published with Little, Brown were each despite (or because of) the blackout a number-one bestseller on all such lists except that of the self-styled "newspaper of record." Unfortunately, for Little, Brown and, in the long run, for me, I was persuaded to leave my Boston publisher for the New York–based Random House; there was also *The New York Review of Books* for whom I'd been writing since their first issue in 1963. As the co-editor, Barbara Epstein, was a friend it made sense to be nearby. In those days Howard and I still lived, despite our first long Roman interlude, on the banks of the Hudson River at Barrytown. I've already noted how hard it is to get out of politics; perhaps I should have added how hard it is to get politics out of oneself; almost as difficult as to get prose out of one's system if one is primarily a novelist reconstructed as a dramatist, something quite other. Each has its satisfactions but the autonomy of the novelist, when not impeded by interested parties, can result in the making of worlds whose anterior form is like that of the primal biblical myth, chaos. For the absolute dramatist like Tennessee the written play is a sort of Eden, lacking only living actors to reenact Adam and Eve and the idea of Lilith as well as the entrance of the snake to start the drama going, rather as God did. The Glorious Bird—the name that I called Tennessee—had caught on with many of his friends and, finally, with him, too. But to acknowledge me as a namer of Beasts diminished him as Supreme author. So, who was *I* then? He found the phrase in a letter to me where I am addressed as "Fruit of Eden," a many-layered image, of course, at whose core there is what the first couple was forbidden ever to sample, knowledge. Thanks to the serpent's crafty malice Eve fell upon knowledge if not wisdom and thus paradise was lost.

THIRTY

————————— ✳ —————————

In rereading and writing about the Bird I am often surprised at how much Christian imagery, Old and New Testament, kept leaking into his work. But then—his sister, Rose, to one side—his maternal grandfather, Dakin, an Episcopal clergyman, was his favorite relative. The old man often joined him in Key West where, in due course, I met him. Recently an archivist at Harvard came across a short story that I had written about the old man, based on an anecdote that Tennessee had told me. When Tennessee was in his adolescence, visiting his grandparents in Mississippi, two men came one day to see the Reverend Dakin. He was, Tennessee later discovered, being blackmailed for an adventure with a boy. Apparently, this was not their first visit but it was the last. The Reverend gave them what he had in the bank and then, when they were gone, he took all his sermons out onto the front lawn and burned them. I found this story hard to forget and it was the eighth and last of the short stories that I was to write in my first phase as a prose writer. When it came time to include it in a volume entitled *A Thirsty Evil*, collegiality required me to show it to the Bird who said I must not use it. Since his grandfather was nearly blind and not apt ever to come across a New Directions anthology of contemporary literature . . . But, the Bird stopped me right there and hissed, "There is *always* Edwina," known to the world as Amanda in *The Glass Menagerie*. I did point out that since she had not sued her son for his portrait of her in that first play she would hardly take up arms to protect her father. But the Bird was firm even after I changed boy to girl. And so the story was obliged to wait half a century for publication by Harvard.

In the Bird's last years I seldom saw him. The barbiturate Nembutal and vodka are a lethal combination and they did his brain no good. But the writing was often still marvelous; also, more adventurous than before. Many critics hoped, even prayed that this was a final falling off from his so unbearable to so many of them greatness. But the talent endured. Medications were only harming, for a time, his memory; he was also having hallucinations: one involved an unpleasant encounter with someone in Spain, only to discover the next day that the offending person had not been in the country. His brother put him away to dry out. "It was not so bad in the bin," the Bird told me later. "I played a great deal of bridge and discovered that some of our best unsung actors are on the television soap operas."

Howard and I were in Rome when the papers revealed that Tennessee Williams, a recent convert to Catholicism, had come there to obtain the Pope's blessing. The story sounded a bit crazy to me but the Bird was always highly dramatic in his effects. We did not see him on that trip but, later, we heard all about the visit from Jesuit friends. Father Navone was an Italo-American professor at Gregorian University. Although Navone had seriously failed to attract me to the Scarlet Woman of Rome (as WASPs still sometimes refer to the original Christian Church) we had remained amiable acquaintances and through him I met many interesting Jesuits—in fact, the most interesting ones were soon to leave the church in the later backlash to the liberalism of Pope John XXIII and the reformations of the Second Vatican Council.

The Glorious Bird and his shifty-eyed dog arrive in Rome to discuss
spiritual matters with the Pope.

Navone offered to be of service to the Bird who repeated that he would indeed appreciate an audience with the Pope (could it have been the arid Montini?). Navone played the Bird like some golden pre-evolutionary fish. The Pope was not possible considering the Bird's tight Roman schedule. But the Black Pope would be happy to receive him. Tennessee was delighted, visualizing a black Pope singing "Ole Man Tiber" and looking like Paul Robeson. Actually the "Black Pope" is the name given the head of the Jesuit order, an order usually at delicate odds with whomever occupies the See of Peter. A time was ordained for this historic meeting. There would be a cocktail party where the Bird could flap about amongst his new co-religionists. Navone, a resourceful well-organized man who had noted the Bird's tendency to vagueness about time and place and, indeed, people, promised to pick up Tennessee in time to take him to the party. The time came. The Bird was napping. He'd just had his daily swim. Drowsily he begged off. He was too exhausted. Tell the Black Pope some other time. Navone rushed to the telephone and rang the Black Pope's secretary, a formidable Englishwoman. She got the Bird on the phone and in a voice more commanding than that of even Edwina told him that Father Navone would presently deliver him, ready or not, to the cocktail party and that he was not allowed to be one minute late.

So it was that the grandson of the Episcopal Reverend Dakin was delivered into the lair of the Black Pope where a dozen or two fascinated Jesuits were waiting for him. The Bird, need I say by now, really hammed it up. As Jesuits crowded about him he intoned, "Ever since I became a Catholic, I feel this astonishing *presence* all about me." (He'd been led into this by, I think, his brother Dakin.) Now the one thing that professionally religious people most hate is listening to laypeople go on about their religious experiences as Bernadette was to discover back in Old World Lourdes. Somewhat taken aback, a Jesuit politely asked, "Is this 'presence' a *warm* presence?"

The Bird fixed him with a beady gaze: "There is no temperature."

"How," asked a helpful Jesuit, "do you write a play?"

"I start," said the Bird, "with a sentence." Presumably, during this dialogue, the Holy Father fled to Avignon.

The last time I saw Tennessee we were on the Kupcinet TV interview program in Chicago. A lady author was discussing her book. The Bird leaned back in his chair to the right of Kupcinet and shut his eyes. He remained like this for quite a while. Finally, the host nudged him. No response. "Tennessee, are you asleep?" "No," said the Bird, "but sometimes I shut my eyes when I am bored."

We parted in the Chicago street below. I noticed he had a rosy butterfly across the bridge of his nose, known to the bibulous French as a *papillon*. We never met again.

THIRTY-ONE

———————— ✳ ————————

Two days ago politics intruded as it has a habit of doing in this bad time. Yes, all times are bad but some times are worse than others. This is one for our country. A Michigan congressman, John Conyers, minority— that is, Democrat—leader of the House Judiciary Committee, went to Ohio with several other members of Congress and a number of staffers to determine whether or not in the late presidential election of 2004 the overexuberant local Republican Party had stolen the election for George W. Bush. The result was a report by Conyers which a Chicago firm published with a preface by me. Yes, Virginia, the election was well and truly stolen and the Conyers team spells it all out in considerable detail. Since the Republican Congress will not allow hearings on what went wrong, Conyers had no recourse other than a book describing in detail how the theft was effected with collusion among high officials and shadowy executives of electronic voting machine companies. Since my name as writer of the preface is on the cover, radio stations with call-in facilities have been ringing me from Arizona to Ohio to Illinois to Texas to—in a few hours from now—New York City. Most of the callers proved to be already suspicious of the election's validity but as they have been given no information by our monolithic media, the Conyers report is the first hard news from the front. Thus far, the report has not been mentioned in the print media. *The New York Times* maintains a sibylline silence as it tends to do when proofs of electoral wrongdoing are nailed, as it were, to the church door. The general liberal (what a meaningless word in the American context!) line has been: no one likes sour grapes. So let's just move on quietly as Gore did in 2000. So what happened next? A blizzard of official lies about Weapons of Mass Destruction. Of collusion between Saddam Hussein and Osama bin Laden, two well-known enemies. The wrecking by Rumsfeld of Iraq and Afghanistan, two countries that had not and could not have done us the slightest harm. Simultaneously as their cities were being knocked down at enormous expense to us, the taxpayers, contracts were being given to the vice president's company, Halliburton, to rebuild those same cities that his colleague at the Defense Department had knocked down. This is a win-win situation for the higher corruption that governs us. Now we are creating air bases in Central Asia to seize Iranian oil reserves? Or, more dangerously, to take on China en route to North Korea or vice versa? Since these so-called neoconservative contingency plans for world conquest will end more soon than late in our destruction one wonders why our media, bought and obedient as they are, cannot see that they are on the wrong side of human history, now more than ever fragile and out of control as we nuclearize space itself and attack nation after nation while silencing those few of our citizens who see what is up ahead for us. Recently one radio caller asked me if it was true that I was the last republican—with a small r. I said I'd better not be since perpetual war for perpetual peace, which is replacing the Republic, will only end in the death of us all. Meanwhile, the glaciers are melting and the seas rise.

Our old original Republic does seem to be well and truly gone. A day or two ago I witnessed the Republican majority of the House Judiciary Committee trash the Democratic minority (which, ironically, actually represents many more millions of Americans than do the "majority" congressional members who represent what Secretary of State William Seward liked to call "the mosquito republics" whose departure in 1860 he quite welcomed, unlike Lincoln, the mystical Unitarian, who chose civil war to keep them attached).

THIRTY-TWO

---- ✳ ----

Those who flew in the early years of the twentieth century were unlike, in many ways, those who did not. Of course most did not live to any great age—they crashed. My youth was filled with family friends wearing neck braces; there were also many premature funerals. My own father was one of the original Army Air Corps pilots trained in 1917. He married the daughter of Senator Gore of Oklahoma and became the first instructor in aeronautics at West Point where I was born in the Cadet Hospital. Bored with peacetime army life, he helped found two small airlines: TAT which metamorphosed into TWA, and the Ludington Line which became Eastern Airlines.

In the mid-thirties he and his friend Amelia Earhart started Northeast Airlines in conjunction with the Boston and Maine Railroad. When Amelia was lost somewhere in the Pacific my father, who had been director of air commerce under FDR, was put by the president in charge of the search. FDR was almost as fond of her as was his wife, Eleanor. A great cloud of conspiracy theories have since surrounded Amelia's disappearance. Thirty years after her disappearance I asked Mrs. Roosevelt whether there was any truth to the stories that Amelia—her friend— had been sent to spy on the Japanese preparations for war in the Pacific and that they had either shot her down or she crash-landed and was made captive.

The veins in Mrs. Roosevelt's left temple often throbbed when she was suddenly moved by emotion recollected. "When the war ended," she said, "I made my own small investigation. As you might suspect. I harassed *everyone* connected with the flight and the search. Certainly, there was nothing of a spying nature about her flight. She simply lost her way trying to find—where was it? Howland Island?"

The last time I saw Amelia we were on the way back from West Point where my father had taken us to see a football game. On the way back to New York City we sat in a compartment of the train as passersby peered through the corridor windows. Amelia was perhaps the world's most famous woman. I asked her what would be the worst part of the trip. The answer was quick. "Africa. If you get forced down in all that jungle with so few cities they could never find you." When I said that the Pacific Ocean looked pretty big to me, she was offhand: "But there are all those islands where you can land. And all those ships passing by." Lately, I've been reading an account of her flight and of how, for the most part, she had routed her flight over land not sea. She had obviously changed her mind about the relative beneficence of overseas flight.

There have been a number of truly imaginative—not to mention dreadful—books about Amelia. One of them was the work of a woman who had convinced herself that Amelia was a nobody invented by a man of genius, her husband, the publicist and publisher George Palmer Putnam. Amelia's marriage to G.P. was a wretched one. He kept her constantly on tour, on view. At one point, she wanted to marry Gene. But he was not romantically inclined and saw her only as a friend, a comrade.

My father's widow, Kit, told me that she had come across a letter

My father, Gene Vidal, director of air commerce, being congratulated by Amelia Earhart for his successful parachute jump; she had preceded him in this game of chicken.

Amelia had written Gene after she had had an accident in California. While her Lockheed Electra plane was being repaired, she'd written an anguished letter all about some sort of emotional problem that she was having. I asked if a name had been mentioned. "Oh, it was so long ago, I forget." I asked Kit if the problem was with a man or a woman. My conventional stepmother frowned at this impropriety. "A man, of course." "So what did you do with the letter?" "I tore it up, naturally. After all, it was no one's business but hers." So there was the final mystery that might have explained what happened. Gene had often speculated that she had deliberately crashed the plane. "She was going through a bad time with G.P.; she was also undergoing some sort of premature menopause." He also said: "The last time I saw her she said she had put me in her will, leaving me this small house she owned because she could trust me to give it to her mother if anything happened to her. So why not, I asked her, just leave it directly to your mother? 'Because,' she said, 'G.P., as widower, would try to get it.' "

I have mentioned how different the early fliers were from other people. There was Lindbergh whose final years were preoccupied with poets like Lao Tse as well as new sorts of procedures to keep hearts alive. I always found the early fliers a bit like a secret society, impatient with us earthbound folk who could never see as much as they saw from their special vertiginous height. Anne Morrow, Lindbergh's wife, wrote highly poetical prose while her passion for the French pilot-writer, Antoine de Saint-Exupéry, produced quantities of mystical prose on both sides until he crashed at sea in the war. Although Gene himself had no mystical or poetic side he was forever a restless inventor-putterer like Lindbergh. Gene's not so secret ambition was to be the Henry Ford of aviation. As director of air commerce he supported any number of prototypes for "flivver" planes to do for flight what Ford's Model T had done for land and at the same affordable price. That's why I took off and landed the Hammond plane at the age of ten in 1936 and was duly immortalized in a Pathé newsreel. Although Gene enjoyed inventing airlines and criss-crossing the country as director, marking out landing fields, he never lost sight of his true goal: the cheap plane that anyone could own. Since the main expense in airplane manufacture was the aluminum fuselage, Gene began to experiment with molded plywood (Vidal Weldwood it was known as); later he tried laminated fiberglass. He never got to make a cheap plane but his molded fiberglass ended up as a mildly lucrative line of trays for a bread company as well as a few thousand dinghies that made occupants itch from the glass.

Lindbergh's daughter has written amusingly of her father's ongoing rage at the poor design of nearly everything, especially flashlights. To be useful, a flashlight must have at least four sides so that it would not, in response to gravity—the flier's nemesis—roll off whatever surface it was resting on. Much of Lindbergh's dialogue on such subjects was very like Gene's, irritation at the compulsive bad design of simple objects and how easy it would be to improve them. A compulsion to improve the utility of everyday objects led to each man's putterings and inventions. Politically, it did not lead much of anywhere except in Lindbergh's case. He was the son of a Swedish American congressman from the Midwest. Like his father, Lindbergh was an isolationist. But he was hardly a pacifist. FDR, who had always been jealous of the "Lone Eagle's" fame, consulted with my father about the uses that could be made of his rival's fame. This is before the America First isolationist movement made it possible to smear such worthy Americans as Norman Thomas, Burton Wheeler, and, not least, Lindbergh as Nazis. Luckily, Gene was apolitical: his only foray into international politics came when, as director of air commerce, he had been invited to Germany for the Olympic Games (he had been a pentathlon silver medalist in the 1920 Olympics at Antwerp). The German airmen were also curious about American air power. But since Gene was a member of the federal government FDR thought, rightly, that his attendance would look like some sort of endorsement of the Nazi regime. So in the end it was Lindbergh who was sent to report on Nazi air power. He was openly shocked by German air superiority over Britain and France and, privately, over the flawed American effort, such as it was. Much was made of the Iron

Cross Göring had slipped him before Lindbergh returned to warn Roosevelt that the Luftwaffe was even more formidable than anyone had suspected and that we would be at a singular disadvantage if we did not begin a buildup in military air power. Lindbergh was busy pushing the B-17 bomber, the so-called Flying Fortress. FDR, despite the malice he bore Lindbergh, knew good advice when he heard it and so, thanks to the Lindbergh reports, in the end it was our air power that won us the war. Meanwhile, politically, FDR could not resist smearing Lindbergh and the other America Firsters as Nazi sympathizers.

THIRTY-THREE

———— * ————

I now realize that I was brought up at the heart of aviation and, simultaneously, through my grandfather, at the then true heart of U.S. politics, the Senate. I lived much of my first seventeen years at Senator and Mrs. Gore's Rock Creek Park house on Broad Branch Road, where I was more and more put to work as a reader to the Senator which I enjoyed, particularly when we were done with the Congressional Record and he would get me to reading Brann the Iconoclast, Robert Ingersoll, and other freethinkers and skeptics, as well as Mark Twain whose complete works were kept not in the attic library with several thousand other books but in the drawing room for a quick fix when "we" read after dinner and Mrs. Gore, relieved of her reading duties, could retreat to her upstairs sitting room and devour serials in *Redbook* and *Ladies Home Companion*. Neither the Senator nor I could understand what she saw in those stories but she had earned her free time or, as the Senator used to chuckle when any of us wearied while reading to him, "Both of Milton's daughters are said to have gone blind reading to him." We were led to believe that it was upon a very high altar indeed that we were being sacrificed. Between grandfather and father I inhabited two worlds, each fascinating to me. I was not interested in my father's so-called legendary career as a jock but his life with Lindbergh and Earhart and the Wright brothers was magical. Also, the serenity of his nature was in benign contrast to my mother's raging nature. I saw her as little as possible; unfortunately, she saw to it that I was not going to spend much time with the Gores or Gene after her marriage to Hugh Dudley Auchincloss, who, through his mother, a Jennings, was a Standard Oil heir. His oleaginous money kept me at schools farther and farther away from Rock Creek and the Gores as well as from Gene, now removed to New York City with a new wife and two new children. Later, when Nina had left Auchincloss, she married her air force general who died early of a blood disease, but by then I was in the army and Gene had been brevetted a major general in the air force to oversee the army's development of new weapons, while his younger brother was a brigadier general in charge of an air force fighter wing stationed in Italy. Gene was distressed at not being given a more combatant role but a coronary thrombosis a few years earlier nearly kept him entirely out of the war. Through father, stepfather, uncle, I got to know, off duty, as it were, many of the great air commanders from Tooey Spaatz to General Doolittle to Pete Quesada to Nate Twining to Uzal G. Ent who took out the Ploesti oil fields (he was also a descendant of one of the original Siamese twins). Many of these generals were startlingly young even to my youthful eye. Like so many of the early fliers they were a race apart. They also tended to political conservatism—but then so did I, not to mention Jack Kennedy who was very much his father's son. My enthusiasm for FDR only developed after the war due to exposure to Eleanor. But I was sometimes shocked to hear generals (*not* the ones noted above) talk about how easy it would be to get rid of Roosevelt through a military coup. Apparently we were fighting the wrong enemy. Stalin not Hitler was the threat. These bull sessions were pretty much just that, fueled by bourbon. After all, none of them was as eloquent as T. P. Gore in denouncing the president. But the Senator never dreamed of a military coup while Gene quite liked the president except for his propensity to lie even when there was no need to. Also, West Point trained its future officers to be accountable for their deeds, unlike presidents who tend cheerfully to outsource blame. When FDR insisted that the army pilots fly the mail despite his director of air commerce's fierce resistance, the result was the death of many pilots as my father had predicted: "We are not trained for flying in all weather. I know. I'm one of them." But FDR ordered the air force into action. After a number of disasters he called in Gene: "Well, Brother Vidal, we seem to have a problem." This was the only time I ever heard Gene express disgust for the president. "I really liked that 'we.' " But Gene was no politician; his fellow West Pointer Eisenhower was. When a similar disaster befell President Eisenhower he sent Jim Hagerty, his press aide, to take the blame for a presidential error. "But," Hagerty whined, "after what I said yesterday to the press corps they'll tear me apart." "Better, my boy," said the smiling Eisenhower, "you than me."

That fliers are—or once were—temperamentally unlike other people is not unnatural. They operated above the earth in every sense. But while the first pilots were uncommonly brave and, often, uncommonly disdainful of us earthbound ants, as flight became more and more universal the differences were less sharp except now in the military where they are beginning to show up in odd ways. Even our slow-witted media is reporting recent problems at the Air Force Academy where Christian evangelicals are now raising hell in Heaven's name by attacking non-Christians with unseemly fervor. Since all of us pay for that academy, and most of us are not Christian zealots, I keep thinking of those generals long ago speaking of the need to send Roosevelt home in order to fight Godless Communism. There now appears to be something potentially dangerous afoot in our military; troops that could very well heed a call to arms of a revolutionary sort.

Between air cadets who are being indoctrinated as Christian soldiers proceeding ever onward and disgusted army reservists vanishing without leave from Iraq and Afghanistan, not to mention the resignations of high-ranking senior officers, our military has been demoralized by the oil-and-gas junta that has seized the government provoking—what? During the Second War Curtis LeMay, commanding general of the B-29s that finished off Japan, was also a voice demanding that we must always be quick to bomb disobedient peoples back into the Stone Age, yet, to his credit, he was one of the senior commanders who begged President Truman *not* to drop the atomic bombs on Hiroshima and Nagasaki. (On the ground that his 20th Air Force had already leveled Japan and he did not want his triumphant devastation obscured by last-minute novelties?)

Gene's younger brother was a charming South Dakota Republican as was, indeed, Gene himself. Although Pick, as General Vidal was known, very much shared the sense of difference that existed between airmen and land-men he was pretty much apolitical except that, postwar, he had bonded with another airman, Barry Goldwater, paladin of far right America. I cannot say I grasped much of this at the time. As, briefly, the "boy pilot," I was a sort of mascot of the fliers as I had been mascot of the Army football team of 1925 which had gone down to serious defeat, no doubt on orders from the sky god.

Pick and Goldwater often flew together once Goldwater became a junior Senator from Arizona and Pick was posted to Washington. Both were brigadier generals in the Air Force Reserve.

The year after I ran for Congress and was labeled a "liberal" because I thought we should recognize the existence of Red China as there seemed to be so many people living there (this is irony), Ralph Graves, editor of *Life* magazine, asked me if I would interview what looked like the next Republican candidate for president against Jack Kennedy in 1964. This meant a lot of reading of speeches on my part but I thought, why not? Goldwater assumed that as the nephew of his friend I'd be friendly even though our chat would be billed as a conversation between a conservative and a liberal. Hard to imagine today such a piece being allowed in what was then perhaps the largest-circulation magazine in the country and devoted, as was its owner, to an ever-expanding American empire and the Christianization of China.

Although I had written in many different genres I had never been a journalist; this meant that I had never been obliged to interview anyone. My uncle thought I would like Barry. I did. But my odd foreboding about those who fly in the wild blue yonder was becoming almost as great as was my fear of those Christians who hanker after that eternal life where Jesus wants them as sunbeams to light the way for the rest of us.

I met Goldwater in his fourth-floor Senate office. I found him a politician of some grace and skill who at that moment was studying the political sky for omens. Would his moment come in the presidential election of 1964 or 1968 or never? There was some evidence that this year he was a divided man, uncertain how to proceed. Camelot was still under construction as we chatted in his office. But the foundations of that future magical kingdom were already shadowed by Kennedy's unsuccessful invasion of Cuba at the Bay of Pigs and by Khrushchev's Berlin Wall. Also, for Goldwater to get the Republican nomination for president in 1964 he would have to take on such powerful "moderate" figures as Nelson Rockefeller.

I took longhand notes. Since Goldwater at his desk was backlit, I described his eyes as dark when fans later wrote me they were blue. He came across as a straightforward unpolished man who held many cranky views which the voters sometimes guiltily identified with but would probably not vote for. Now, as I write, the Cheney-Bush junta is reenacting the Goldwater agendum. I wrote in *Life* how "Goldwater, reluctantly, realizes that Social Security is here to stay—it is too late to take it away—but he thinks the program should be voluntary and certainly not enlarged to include medical care for the aged or anything else. He favors breaking off diplomatic relations with the Russians; he wants to present them wherever possible with a take-it-or-leave-it, peace or war attitude. He noted sadly that when conservative true believers in the Republican Party come to nominate a candidate for president they invariably choose a liberal or moderate candidate." So I proposed: "Why not start a third party?" He was brisk. "If I thought it would work, I might. But I don't know. Third parties never get off the ground in this country . . . For one thing conservatism is pretty divided . . . No. A political party can only start around a strong individual." He looked past me at the bust of Lincoln on the mantelpiece; his jaw set. "Like Lincoln." Jack Kennedy very much enjoyed my piece. "For me he's the dream Republican candidate, while Nelson Rockefeller could be trouble."

I ended my piece with Cicero's warning to a fellow political adventurer, in a falling year of the Roman republic: "I am sure you understand the political situation into which you have . . . no, not stumbled but stepped; for it was by deliberate choice and by no accident that you flung your tribunate into the very crisis of things; and I doubt not that you reflect how potent in politics is opportunity, how shifting the phases, how incalculable the issue of events, how easily swayed are men's predilections, what pitfalls there are and what insincerity in life." When this was published June 9, 1961, Henry Luce complimented the editor on its brilliance, adding, "I never again want to see a piece like that in *Life*." I gather he never did. Goldwater fans were angry because when I had noted that as a public-relations man for his family's department store, he had also invented a line of men's boxer shorts decorated with red ants.

I saw Goldwater several times after our 1961 interview. Once at the Cow Palace in San Francisco when he was nominated for president. Southwestern U.S. had converged on that elegant city. Lady golfers with dangerous-looking tans led his claque. They were also in place to keep the immoral New Yorker Nelson Rockefeller from being nominated. When Nelson tried to speak to the convention they howled him down. Had he not notoriously got rid of his old wife in favor of a younger woman who had been married to *one of his employees*? For some reason this act of *droit de seigneur* caused them to shriek like banshees in unison as they shouted their fearsome epithet for him: "*Lover!*" He fled the stage. Meanwhile cowboy-style Southwestern males wearing alligator boots and Stetson hats were busy chasing the television anchorpersons from the convention floor and back up to their control rooms high above the convention. Since I was covering the convention for Westinghouse I too joined in the flight which somehow drove Huntley and

Brinkley and the rest of us through an endless kitchen. Apparently, the rich had had it. They weren't going to take the likes of us anymore. They also were in no mood to respect their former president, Eisenhower, who was nearly booed down until the crowd finally got a look at his scarlet face and raging eyes. One furious look from the ancient lion shut them all up. He said something and then turned his back on a people he'd never much cared for.

Before I abandoned the convention I chatted with a Mr. White in charge of Goldwater's press. With me were Norman Mailer and Douglas Kiker. All that I can recall of what any of us said was when Mr. White referred, apropos some recent poll, to "the whiny American people." This was a truly up-front campaign. Which made it possible, forty years later, for us to enjoy so many recent radical events as well as wild pre-emptive wars, despite our whines. Some years ago at the Los Angeles airport, as I walked down a corridor toward the baggage area, I saw a very old wispy man pushing a sort of cart with a suitcase on top of it. There was Barry Goldwater, quite alone. The trumpets had ceased. Oddly I was not yet done with the family. In 1982, curious to see what was going on in the political world, I entered the Democratic California primary for U.S. Senate. There were nine contestants led by the sitting governor Jerry Brown. After two terms as governor and an attempt or two at the presidency Jerry was weak while the other candidates, a mayor of Fresno, a state legislator from Orange County were not formidable. On the Republican side it was agreed by all that the senatorial candidate would be Barry Goldwater Junior, a member of the House of Representatives. The name was still magic in ultraconservative circles.

I spent a year campaigning up and down a state that was larger than most first-world nations. The part of politics that most politicians often hate I liked the most: the crowds, and hearing new things. Unfortunately, the first thing press and pollsters want to know is how much money have you raised? Since I am not able to ask people for money, I had to admit very little. More to the point, I could not say that if I wanted to I could use my own money which was more than enough to win a

San Francisco: We were in the Cow Palace commenting upon the Republican Convention for Westinghouse. From left to right: historian Allan Nevins, someone from Westinghouse TV, myself, and Marc Connelly, a cheerful playwright whose bald pate had recently been dented when a chair in Manhattan fell on him from above. At the moment the convention delegates are safely behind us. Later we were chased through a labyrinth of kitchens along with other TV worthies thought to be hostile to the candidate from the Southwest, Barry Goldwater.

Senate seat that year. I was counting on two things: Brown was weak and was bound to lose if not in the primary in the general election, while Barry Goldwater Junior was thought to be nothing more than a brand name. During the primary period he and I made appearances at a few candidate meetings. I remember going downstairs with him in an elevator. The press had been making fun of him. He appealed to me: "I don't think I'm so dumb, do you?" "No dumber than the rest," I reassured him. Then one day, quite suddenly, he took himself out of the race and his place as Republican front-runner was taken by a powerful politician, Pete Wilson, the mayor of San Diego. I might beat Brown but I could not beat Wilson considering all the money behind him. From that moment on I simply went through the motions. Finally, in the field of nine, I came in second with half a million votes. The last I heard of the campaign was seeing Wilson on TV saying: "Jerry Brown wouldn't debate Gore Vidal but he'll debate me." I never bothered to find out if this memorable confrontation ever took place. Wilson won the Senate seat in order to become governor, an inscrutable choice unless you scrutinize what was actually happening. In subsequent years Jerry and I became political allies. I helped him with speeches when he ran for president against Clinton. Some years before he had entered, at the last minute, a presidential primary against Carter. Suddenly he was winning state after state. Finally, when he won Maryland, thought to be Carter territory, nothing more happened. "Why," I asked him later, "didn't you go on to the end?" "Because it was already too late. I'd entered the race too late."

"You knew you couldn't win the nomination when you started?"

"Yes. I knew all along." Jerry has an odd crooked smile which he suddenly deployed. "Do you think I'm neurotic?" he asked, much amused.

Now he is running for state attorney general. "It's the only job where you can actually do something useful. My father always said it was the one time he was really happy in politics. The governorship is just endless photo ops," he added.

And so highly suitable for professional actors. Democracy!

THIRTY-FOUR

———————— ✳ ————————

Gene Vidal died in February 1969 at a hospital in Inglewood not far from where his last surviving sister, Margaret, lived. He had a cancer of the kidney. He was well-looked-after by a cousin-surgeon and by Kit, his wife.

Now, in June 2005, I am sent the galleys of Joan Didion's *The Year of Magical Thinking* which describes her husband, John's, death in New York City.

It is hard to think of that quaking burning Pacific littoral without thinking of Joan who is the quintessential native: several generations of her family have flourished in the Sacramento area and few seem to have defected, including Joan and her husband, John Gregory Dunne, who, even when they did move to New York, always seemed to be somehow organically connected with her state.

It was at Malibu where I was first taken to see them by Jean Stein whom I had known since she was a child and I was an eighteen-year-old soldier soon to be shipped out to the Aleutian Islands. By the time I ate the Portuguese fish dish cooked by Joan it was some years after I'd re-turned from the Bering Sea. My mother, Nina, and Jean's mother, Doris, had been passionately busy with their joint war work in the Polo Lounge of the Beverly Hills Hotel. Now once the war was done, I saw the Didion-Dunnes from time to time. He was a splendid gossip in the low key while she had, according to that great transatlantic gossip, Ali Forbes, "the most endearing scowl."

At the time of our Malibu meeting I was a novelist in Hollywood, writing television plays for CBS's new studio on Fairfax Avenue. Even so, I was not often in California in those days but I often thought of see-ing the Didion-Dunnes particularly after they abruptly moved on to New York City and left their house in Brentwood to be quickly torn down as things tend to be in that least permanent of places. Joan records her grief when she finally saw what had been done to their house. Now, John has just died in New York. Joan goes on. The Polo Lounge in the Beverly Hills Hotel also goes on unchanged and, some-times, in the large booth opposite the entrance to the bar, I can just make out the ghosts of those two Stakhanovite war-workers, Nina and Doris, two ladies plainly invented by Dawn Powell, to cheer our boys on to victory while exchanging endless secrets and drinking vodka.

THIRTY-FIVE

———————— ✳ ————————

Until the end, Howard and I kept on making plans for future trips. The one that we were most looking forward to was aboard the Radisson line, starting from near home at Salerno and then on to the Greek islands and the Turkish coast. In exchange for our passage, I'd lecture on Greece and the islands, putting me in competition with my august friend Gough Whitlam, onetime prime minister of Australia and a classicist who had been doing pretty much the same thing for another line. Unfortunately, we never made that trip to the Greek islands but at least, years earlier, Howard and I had sailed the Aegean in a caique with Paul Newman whose wife, Joanne Woodward, jumped ship at the first stop and flew to London to attend the theater. Meanwhile, our arrival at each of a dozen islands was heralded by youthful voices shouting, in unison, POLE. NOO . . . MUN! How they knew we were aboard so nondescript a boat restores one's belief in the Sirens who infested those waters when Ulysses himself sailed by. We also encountered some rather grim sirens when we put into port at Mykonos. A tall Giacometti-style woman vaulted aboard to introduce herself to Paul as a Hohenzollern princess of Prussia. She was swollen with ouzo not to mention imperial airs. "Get rid of her," Paul kept muttering to me and Howard. We did our best but her long imperial limbs seemed made of fettuccine: we could never get a polite grip on her. Suddenly, this self-styled heiress to Frederick the Great slithered free of us and rushed into Paul's stateroom where she relieved herself of what seemed to be a gallon of ouzo on his bunk. With that, Howard, who had a strong managerial side and spoke sailors' Italian, shouted for the police to rescue POLE NOO MUN which they did. The imperial princess put up a fight worthy of her great ancestor Der Alte Fritz but she was soon shore-bound as our skipper weighed anchor and got us around the island. For a long time Mykonos gossip, I'm told, spoke of a royal romantic quarrel aboard our ship the *Helena Pente* while in port. Luckily, the princess proved to be our last perhapsburg.

The next morning we awakened to a science-fiction world. At the center of the island of Santorini—sometimes called Thera—there is a deep crater filled with blue-black water. Rising from the water were the sides of the volcano whose spectacular explosion in 1520 BC allegedly ended the Minoan civilization on nearby Crete and destroyed a fairly glittering civilization at Santorini.

Howard, Paul, and I rode donkeys to the top of what was left of the volcano. Archaeologists were only beginning their excavations of surprisingly well-preserved modern-looking buildings. Some still had their walls, murals, and roofs while tomatoes were in full bloom on the winding path to the top of the mountain. These tomatoes proved to be our breakfast.

I had read a great deal about the eruption of Santorini before we arrived in the obsidian black crater of what had been the original volcano. The capital of the Minoan empire was Knossos on nearby Crete and as most of the Cretan palaces and villages including Knossos had been in ruins until Arthur Evans, a renowned archaeologist, who was perhaps too much school of Walt Disney, had undertaken extensive restorations which gave one a sense of what Walt Disney himself might have done

Paul Newman and I in 1961 on the island of Delos where the god Apollo was born. Here we are saluting what is left of one of the monuments.

had he been assigned to so vast a project. Purists hated the result. I was neutral because I had nothing to compare Evans's work to. But Santorini the day that Howard, Paul, and I arrived at noon was very much like Herculaneum, the lava-buried city south of Naples where archaeologists are still restoring parts of the city to what it had looked like originally, right down to charred wood furniture and elaborate carbonized venetian blinds.

Santorini, a thousand years older than Herculaneum and Pompeii, is an even more vivid look at the past exactly as it was when the top of the mountain blew off and a city was smothered while villages were preserved with all sorts of food on their tables, excepting the tomato, a late arrival from Virginia.

Since as a writer I've ranged about from fifth century BC to most of our relatively brief American story I am quite used to the plunge into the past, often prompted by newly revealed ruins. At fourteen when sent off to the most uncongenial Los Alamos Ranch School I ignored as much as was possible the horses not to mention most of my fellow students (William Burroughs had come and gone by the time I arrived). And so I was left with the school library where, to the horror of the teachers, I read my way through the Yale edition of Shakespeare; then, with pick and shovel, I took over a nearby Indian Pueblo ruin and excavated the original ground level in the course of a season to the bewilderment, commingled with loathing, of an ahistorical faculty chosen for their hearty Theodore Rooseveltian love of the great wild west outdoors. I've disliked TR, the spiritual founder of Los Alamos, to this day. Happily my excavations exempted me from mindless games. Then, after the Easter vacation of 1940 I went "home" to the Potomac Palisades manse of Mr. and Mrs. Hugh D. Auchincloss where I told her that the headmaster of the Ranch School was a remarkably busy pederast. Nina chose to disbelieve me by which time I had no interest at all in her opinion on any subject. More to the point, that was the spring when the Nazis occupied France and we were flung into history with a vengeance. Luckily, Gene also hated Los Alamos, particularly the Auchincloss-size bills that he had to pay, and so I was shipped off to Exeter, a place in real time. My last look at my "dig" was emblematic of all art. What I had so painstakingly dug up had been crudely filled in with desert dust. I still retained some pieces of ancient pottery.

But on a vivid blue day overlooking the sea there were few tourists at Santorini so one could wander about in rooms unoccupied for several thousand years. While Howard and Paul drank beer at a taverna nearby, I was pacing off rooms. Measuring doors—how short the people must have been. Every now and then I had a fleeting glimpse of one of them just around a corner only to find that he had been painted on a wall. But what had gone on in the house? Had it doubled as a shop? Thus the compulsive historical mind feeds itself on potsherds. And not much else. At that time Santorini had both too much history and too little . . . There were those who believed that it was Atlantis similarly destroyed; others believed that mainland Crete had been Atlantis. Before one chose either tale there would have to be some overarching holistic reason not yet revealed by the archaeological shovel. Or a flash of intuition. But none came, and so we sailed away on the *Helena* and none of us ever came back and a world starting to form in my mind simply aborted, as indeed had the "real" one under the volcano.

My father's death was celebrated by a perfectly emblematic event: the first Americans had landed on the moon. Father and son equally gasped as a hollow voice told us that this was a small step for a man but a giant step for mankind. There had been much discussion about what sort of a step it would prove to be: there were those who maintained that the moon was enveloped in a shroud of dust and that the first man to set foot on the surface would promptly disappear from view. But he did not. The dust was only a few inches thick framed by the black sky that enfolded this sterile globe about which our race had speculated since we first left the primordial ooze for the tumultuous planetary air that, as we stared at the television set, it looked as if we might soon abandon for the oxygenless lunar landscape stepping-stone, if nothing else, to outer space and the ultimate encounter with the Big Bang, our true origin where, at last, we could meet ourselves and—merge? Or would time—our time at least—have a stop as a circular eternity swallows us up?

The physics and metaphysics were fascinating to contemplate. Unfortunately we were given little time to contemplate this greatest of events. Pentagon machinery had overtaken the moon; we had surpassed the Communists was the general theme of the celebration of what was happening. The whole world was ours—and other worlds, too. Gene, who disliked boasting, switched off the sound. But I was in a mood for boasting. I told him that after Kennedy was elected president he asked a number of us to write him what should be the principal goals of his administration: the exploration of space, I declared. Science fiction has a loyal audience. The Russians had already got into space with Sputnik. Rather cynically, I had noted that since it was generally agreed that most earthly problems were not going to be solved by the governments now in place a total break with the planet would not only divert everyone's attention but literally open new vistas.

Gene was amused: "I can just see the wars over who gets the mineral rights to the moon." But he was delighted to be still alive at that moment. He liked to recall how as director of air commerce he had launched an aerial salute to the Wright brothers involving most of the aircraft in the nation. "I always knew we were headed for the moon and beyond but I never thought that I would live to see it." He did by some months.

He had been struck at New Year's by an odd pneumonia. X-rays revealed lung cancer. For someone who neither smoked nor drank and could still fit into his West Point uniform Gene was given to a host of illnesses, some quite mysterious. The fact that the lung cancer disappeared in a week or two meant that one of his mystery ailments had struck. When lungs were found to be clear, his mood changed to normal. To celebrate he smoked a small cigar, his first in several decades. But he resolutely refused his doctor-cousin's excellent dry martini whose ingredients and shaker were always close to hand thanks to a well-trained nurse. Finally, the lung cancer made a mysterious brief reappearance. Then the ultimate non-mystery: he had cancer of the kidney and must be promptly operated upon. It was I who drank our doctor-cousin's perfect martini. When the day of the operation broke, as always, at dawn to suit some arcane hospital timetable he set aside his chronic hypochondria (because he knew this was not a mystery but the real thing). He joked with the hospital functionary: Were they certain that they were going to remove the right kidney? His wife, Kit, an edgy woman in daily life, was endlessly serene in crisis. He was part-sedated when I left the hospital room. I waved at him—neither liked to be touched. He gave an odd gulp. On the television set a shadowy Richard Nixon was busy thanking Buzz and Biff and Joe, what sounded more like an Eskimo dog pack than astronauts far from earth. I slipped away.

As usual with him, the operation was a success. They had got all the cancer, they said. I didn't know then that they seldom do. But I had now entered cancer valley, as I think of California. Thanks to the relentless atomic testing to the east of Los Angeles in Nevada we are all generously exposed to radiation. A final visit to the hospital room. The curious gray-yellow eyes were bright; he was puffing a slender cigar—this was not addiction or even pleasure but an odd defiance. I murmured to my stepmother I thought it a bad idea. She was rather hard: "It's too late now." I tried to hush her up. Surprisingly, she said, "It makes no difference—he's still knocked out—he can't understand you." He actually laughed. "Of course I can. After all, I've still got cancer." I'll never know if she was right and at the conscious level of his brain he was already elsewhere or that he was compos mentis and did not seem to care what turn the conversation took.

A week or two later he was up and around: a full recovery I was told. He was also taking a variation of Dr. Niehans's miracle sheep placenta, the same concoction that kept Somerset Maugham in not so rude health for far longer than anyone liked. I flew back to Rome.

The Roman winter of 1969–1970 was dismal for me due to Gene's condition. He was being kept alive by the shots from Switzerland. During this glum period I seem to have published an essay a week, mostly in *The New York Review of Books* which had superseded, as predicted by Edmund Wilson, *The New York Times Book Review*. Howard and I had also rented a small flat in Klosters, a village in the canton of Graubünden, a few miles from Feldkirch in Austria, the town where my great-grandfather in 1848 had begun his emigration to the United States after first marrying Emma Carolina von Hartmann de Traxler of Lucerne. They settled in Racine, Wisconsin, sometimes referred to as Swisscon-sin. It is said that the first member of our family to arrive in the United States, Eugen Fidel Vidal, had been the only Swiss immigrant to fail in the cheese business in Wisconsin, but as he was, I know from docu-ments, a graduate of the University of Lausanne, I still don't know if he was actually a medical doctor as he had claimed to be. We do know that not long after settling his wife, Emma, one son, and two daughters in Racine he vanished for twenty years. Since these years coincided with our Civil War I assume that having left his native Austria to avoid con-scription he felt no overpowering passion to join Mr. Lincoln's army. During his absence, Emma supported her children by translating from newspapers and magazines for the American press. She was fluent in German, French, and Italian. She brought up her children with many Old World airs and graces. She also kept a casket filled with family coats of arms necessary to prove that she was a true member of the lower no-bility and so eligible for membership in various grand societies.

In due course, Eugen returned with no tale to tell about his disap-pearance. One family story has it that Emma promptly put him in the poorhouse. But some of the cousinage have found their gravestones, side by side, in a Catholic cemetery at Racine. Her place of birth is given as Carthage. This was the best Racine could do with Cartagena where she had been born, thanks to the Peninsular War: She was a daughter of the Swiss captain of the Spanish king's guard. Gene had no interest in history, his own or anyone else's, so what he might have been told by his grandparents and others he had long since forgotten by the time I started asking questions. One aunt recalled having seen Eugen Fidel who spoke with a heavy German accent and every evening wore a frayed red velvet jacket. I have two small boxes containing slips of paper addressed to him by classmates from Lausanne, wishing him luck, presumably in the New World. I could find no references to medicine or any other profession in these slips of paper. I did discover that his maternal grandfather had been burgermeister of Feldkirch while family legend has it that Emma had had a falling out with the Jesuits who effectively governed Feldkirch from their vast monastery on a hill overlooking the town. The fight had to do with a contested piece of property, which she lost, thus explaining an anticlerical streak in the entire family ever since.

Along with numerous essays I was novel-writing again, in longhand on yellow legal pads which were then typed up by an eccentric American woman who had worked for a time for Lawrence Durrell and had many stories to tell, mostly about his apparently prodigious capacity in the kitchen and at the dinner table. Briefly, she had been involved with a Jewish American and they had moved to Tel Aviv, where she had expected a brilliant intellectual life like nineteenth-century Prague. "Instead," she grumbled, "it's just another hopelessly incompetent Mediterranean city like Rome." In the end she moved back to Rome and a lifetime of irritability. Since I had no expectations of Rome other than its history, in which I was marinated from what seems like birth, what bored her enchanted me. But in the end I, too, was bored and so was Howard. From Klosters I did some research in the files of St. Stephen's Church. Although birth and death certificates were missing, there was a full record of everyone's marriages. Apparently in the 1580s we moved on south to Friuli, to a village called Forni a Voltri where we lived until, as the record bleakly puts it, the father of Eugen Fidel returned home to "the empire" . . . to Feldkirch where the Vidals had a prosperous pharmaceutical business with a number of outlets including, I assume, Forni a Voltri and Venice itself. When my father died he left me a stained-glass medallion with a picture of a bearded man wearing a hat. Back of him are jewel-like vases containing drugs. A man wearing a sword waits patiently for his fix. The man at the counter is my ancestor Caspar Vidall and the date is 1589. On my first visit to Feldkirch I visited the shop with its vast cellars where every sort of chemical had been stored. My last trip to Feldkirch revealed that the tradition-loving Austrians had torn down Vidalhaus, built in 1300. I did learn that another interesting family had lived there in our time: the Frei family who later emigrated to Chile where two members became president. The medallion which has passed from eldest son to eldest son since the 1500s is all that is left of our time in the Austrian empire.

The Freis had, I am told, the best pastry shop in Feldkirch. I suggested to a dull biographer that he write the current Frei for information but, alas, because I had begun my first memoir with an ironic joke about memoirs being "tissues of lies" he assumed that everything I'd written in my own memoir was a lie to be relentlessly probed by his resolute dullness. The biographer, himself Jewish, was positive we were Spanish Jews who had converted in the fourteenth century at the time the family business began in Feldkirch. I thought this romantic and thought no more about it. Then on October 2, 1990, one Robert E. Wachs wrote: "Dear Mr. Vidal, I came upon something which may be of interest to you. I was walking through the Montparnasse cemetery in Paris last week, and saw in the Jewish section of that cemetery a gravestone for Vidal-Bouvier. The name struck me because I seem to recall that you are related to Jacqueline Kennedy Onassis, but assumed that Bouvier was Catholic, and that neither Vidal nor Bouvier was Jewish."

I've always known that Vidal was a name Jews took in troubled times since the Latin root *vita vitalis* for Vidal in Italian means "life," as does the Hebrew *Chaim*. Though my quarrel with Bobby K. had ended my friendship with Jackie I couldn't resist sending her a copy of the letter with the note: "I'd heard about me but not about you." I fear she did not sprint to the letter box to confess. Now my far-flung readers have come up with a more plausible origin of name and family. I'd always taken it for granted that we were Romanish people placed in the Alps by Tiberius to defend the frontiers. The Romano Raetians are the smallest

Since the death of the apothecary Caspar Vidall, this stained-glass medallion from 1589 has descended from eldest son to eldest son until 1969 when my father died and the medallion came to me. Caspar presumably lived in Vidalhaus in Feldkirch, Vorarlberg (Austria), where he can be seen at work preparing some sort of potion for a carriage-trade gentleman. My one visit to Vidalhaus was in the 1960s and I was struck by the huge cellars where the drugs from a network of such shops extended across the then Austro-Hungarian empire all the way down to Friuli and Venice. The family Vital was Romanisch and a branch still lives in the Engadin. Under fascism Mussolini insisted that the mountain folk add vowels to their names so Vital became Vitale; the "t" had become a "d" as early as the 1580s. Also at home in Vidalhaus was a family of pastry makers called Frei; they emigrated to Chile where, in recent years, two of them became president.

Swiss minority with their own difficult Latinate dialect honored by Swiss law. Recently, I received a letter from a reader in Sent, a town near Saint Moritz in the Engadine valley. Mr. Not Vital wrote, "I was astounded and very proud to read that you are a Raetoromansh, so am I. During lunch with my mother here in Sent, I told her that your grandfather was Felix Vidal. She looked at me: 'Fila Vidal [Fila is Felix in English] left Sent for America.'" Unfortunately, my grandfather Felix Vidal was born in Racine, Wisconsin, the son of Eugen Fidel Vidal born in Feldkirch in 1820 who emigrated in 1848. How best to claim so exotic a heritage!

THIRTY-SIX

——————— ✳ ———————

While still living in Largo Argentina we lived a fairly ordered social life. Our usual fairly disordered life simply meant we'd have dinner with each other at a trattoria or with one or another of friends in the city or sometimes with passersby who'd ring up like Saul Bellow or F. W. Dupee, friends and acquaintances from our Hudson life now drawing to a close. Actually, an ordered social life was nearly impossible for me: it meant writing down in a book invitations accepted and then, in due course, honoring them. This obliged us to see the same people over and over again. One evening as I was dressing to go out to dinner at Mimi Pecci-Blunt's palace opposite the Campidoglio I got the inevitable telephone call: "Gene is worse. Only the shots are keeping him alive. He's also been hallucinating. Just now he said, 'If I don't get out of this motel soon I'll become extinct.'" Hardly his usual language. My stepmother was herself somewhat formal in manner; she had been brought up by her mother in Beijing in the thirties and she recalled that period as the most magical of her life. An early boyfriend had been a son of the historian Arnold Toynbee; the young man's romantic suicide seemed always to be, somehow, at the edge of her memory unlike her long-absent wealthy father, Owen Roberts, who had separated from her mother. Gene had brought father and daughter together. When the old man died, his daughter inherited an eighteenth-century house on a crater lake overlooking Hartford, Connecticut, a tall mountain almost entirely surrounded by the Alsop family, one of whom was Joe—the political columnist and devotee of empire as well as some sort of relative to "Uncle T" as Theodore Roosevelt was known to him: Uncle T had characteristically presented his infant relative with the tooth of a saber-tooth tiger, always on conspicuous display in Joe's Georgetown house.

I quizzed my stepmother about the various doctors and their reports. How far had the cancer spread? Apparently, to the brain. She was waiting for me to say something and I was waiting, in my turn, for her to say the inevitable which turned out to be, "Shall we stop the Swiss injections." A curtain was suddenly coming down on Gene. As I talked into the telephone all I could see was a man taking a step on the dusty moon. And so it was, without words, we agreed to stop the medicine. Ordinarily, I would have talked this over with Howard but he'd already gone to dinner with friends. Then I walked the short distance to the Pecci palace; went to the wrong door; waited and waited. Finally I was let in. Dinner had begun without me. Mimi was polite, even droll. I made a mumbled excuse, thinking of Proust, of Swann, of Madame Verdurin who was, somehow—the original one, that is—related to Mimi who was herself a niece to Pope Leo XIII. The next day while I was struggling with a letter of apology to Mimi a footman arrived with a letter from her which combined Proustian tact with the Thomist wisdom of her uncle Pecci. And that is how it was I entered man's usual state, as an orphan. But I am ahead of my story since my mother did not die until 1978, but as I had not seen her in the twenty years previous to her death, at the end it was as if we had never known each other. She had attacked Howard who had genuinely liked her, which was more than I had ever done, and so I had told her that I never wanted to see her again and never did. I was startled at how many ladies of my acquaintance were horrified when they read this account in the first volume of these memoirs. Obviously, a new epoch of mother worship had been ushered in by . . . Freud? Fannie Farmer? I've yet to read any criticism of George Washington for his bad relations with his mother or even Ernest Hemingway. But a sea change occurred in the twentieth century and mothers are automatically exempted from all blame if my lady friends are to be believed.

Meanwhile, a happy voluntary mother-daughter relationship was being acted out each winter and sometimes summer, too, at Klosters in Switzerland. Salka Viertel was the widow of a well-known German film director and mother of the writer Peter Viertel. A sometime actress and screenwriter, Salka had been chosen by Greta Garbo to be her mother. Salka lived down the street from Howard and me and next to the small flat where Garbo stayed; she did her yoga exercises on the balcony to the amazement of the villagers who had no idea just who Frau Garbo was.

Thanks to my Aleutianized left knee I could never ski well but cross-country skiing was possible as well as long walks beside the Silvretta River. Or even the longer walk to Davos where the characters in Thomas Mann's *The Magic Mountain* died of tuberculosis while immersed in philosophical tautologies.

Garbo had become very fond of our Australian terrier, Rat. "But it is such a brutal name for him so I shall call him Ratski." And so each morning at about eight she would come by our flat and Ratski would rush out into the street to greet her. Then I would join them for our morning walk beside the nearby Silvretta River. On the walk Rat took charge, as always. We went only where he wanted to go.

Irwin Shaw and his wife were longtime friends of Garbo and warned us never to discuss her film career. As it turned out, that was what she most wanted to talk about. She recalled every detail of every movie, including the names of the grips. "I learn my bad English from them," she said, reminding us that she had been a star of silent movies and the whole world had wondered whether or not the glamorous

A last summer at Klosters. Garbo is sixty-five. I could never get her to come back to Ravello where she had spent her "honeymoon" with the conductor Leopold Stokowski only to be driven away by a newsreel cameraman in the bushes who boasted ever after of his great coup. One did not grieve when he was later shot by the Mafia.

voiceless Swede could make the transition to talking pictures, something her co-star John Gilbert had failed to do. Not only did she like to talk about the old days but she wanted to know what MGM was like so many years later. She also had a number of ribald stories that she enjoyed telling and retelling. Although she had been queen of MGM she was not above keeping an eye on the minor stars at court. For some reason the thought of the singer Jeanette MacDonald caused all the stars at Metro to start laughing while Judy Garland would burst into a flat-filled version of Jeanette's signature song "San Francisco." Doubtless, it had something to do with the old-fashioned operettas that Jeanette appeared in, along with her co-star Nelson Eddy fondly known as "the singing capon." One story that Garbo liked to tell: Jeanette was married to an actor called Gene Raymond, an amiable sort who appeared in my film *The Best Man*. One morning Raymond was playing tennis with a coach while Jeanette arrives, in a picture hat (one starts decorating the scene when these magical figures appear in a narrative), a basket of freshly cut roses on one arm while trilling an aria from *Naughty Marietta*. As she enters the house, she reminds her husband that lunch will soon be ready. Raymond invites the pro to lunch but he says, "I'm all sweaty and I didn't bring any other clothes." Gene Raymond says, "Go up to my bathroom. There's a shower and plenty of clothes your size." So the tennis pro goes into the house. Meanwhile, Jeanette, weary from her decorative labors, is putting roses into vases. Then, as she passes her husband's bathroom, she hears the shower running. She slips into the bathroom, pokes her hand into the shower stall, firmly grips the pro's genitals and sings, fortissimo, "Ding, dong, Daddy, Don't be late for lunch!" then she resumes her journey along the corridor only to come face-to-face with her husband. By this time Garbo would be roaring with laughter, her right hand twitching convulsively.

Much has been written about her androgynous appeal. While she was worshipped as a goddess by L. B. Mayer the longtime master of the studio, they both were alert to the basis of her popularity. Women loved her movies—she suffered; she was beautiful in a way few people are. Yet she was not popular with American men who preferred the Betty Grable type. The important money earned from a Garbo picture came largely from Europe. When World War Two put an end to the European market, Garbo nicely let MGM off the contractual hook. She would take a vacation until the war was over. It is said L.B. wept with gratitude. Contrary to legend she did not intend to retire. When the war was over Walter Wanger prepared a script for her based on Balzac's *La Duchesse de Langeais*, to be released by RKO. Garbo got as far as the wardrobe test, a subtle way for the studio to see if she still looked like Garbo. She did. I've seen the test. But then she was only in her thirties. Unfortunately, the studio was bought by an aviation colleague of my father who promptly canceled the Garbo movie. It is a pity that Scorsese in his film about Howard Hughes left out the only thing that Hughes would ever be famous for. So shocked was Garbo by this abrupt rejection that she never came close to making another film. She was also very rich and somewhat lazy.

In Klosters she had a simple routine. She would collect the morning paper then get back into bed for a fat-free breakfast while reading the newspaper and the various *Silver Screen* movie magazines she had collected during the week. She kept up with all the new stars though I can't imagine she saw many of their pictures, but when it came to Fabian's romantic life she was au courant.

When someone sent me a large tin of Beluga caviar Howard decided to give a small party just for us, the Irwin Shaws, and Garbo. At the last moment Irwin rang to ask if he could bring the journalist Martha Gellhorn. I'd always liked her writing and felt sympathetic to anyone who'd been married to Hemingway. The small party went off well. Garbo arrived early and promptly put on Howard's blazer. She liked dressing up in men's clothes. She also liked to refer to herself in masculine terms. "Where is the little boys' room" was a favorite expression. It was Ina Claire, the urbane comedienne from Broadway, who went to the little boys' room right after Garbo had vacated it and, yes, the toilet seat had been left up.

THIRTY-SEVEN

———————— ✳ ————————

Never rent, buy—if you can. This bit of antebellum lore I learned from my grandparents. Around 1946 while traveling through Guatemala I found a sixteenth-century monastery in the earthquake-ruined city of Antigua. For something like $3,000 I bought it with my meager earnings from a first novel. An American architect who lived in the town agreed to restore the building if I allowed him to live in it. This proved to be a successful arrangement. But after two or three years I was ready to move on; and did. Europe had, as they say, opened up again and I started traveling seriously. But I knew that sooner or later I'd be obliged to buy another house. Why? The books I kept accumulating—in which I resembled Senator Gore whose houses in Washington kept getting bigger as he acquired more and more books. I was the same. In due course, I sold the Guatemala house. Later, back in New York, I was invited to lunch by a transatlantic lady Alice Pleydell-Bouverie. She had spent the war years in London and then came back to New York with her children. She was to the end more English than American and lived in a sort of English manor house near the village of Rhinebeck on the Hudson River not far from her endlessly irritable and irritating brother Vincent Astor who owned much of New York City. Meanwhile, Howard and I settled in a small apartment over the Dover food shop in Lexington Avenue where I started to write plays for television. Alice lent us the odd chair or two. We also visited her at Rhinebeck where she was assembling a life for herself much like the one she had known in England, centered on the ballet, where she had been a considerable patron thanks to her friendship with Frederick Ashton. She resumed much the same role in New York but never ceased to long for prewar England. She had stored away a vast amount of furniture to be used when it came time to furnish her English house but, like a Chekhovian heroine, she never went back to live in England. Happily, a stream of British friends came to visit her at Rhinebeck or stayed in Manhattan at her brother Vincent's hotel the Saint Regis.

On one visit to Alice's house she took us for a drive through the countryside to see a beautiful Greek Revival house built in 1820 with columns and an octagonal library, the work of A. J. Davis. A lawn extended from portico down to the Hudson River. There were also three acres of willow and locust trees as well as a small island in the river. My television work paid, barely, for the house—some $16,000. On the other hand, I had no money to furnish the place. Alice allowed me to use some of the furniture intended for the London house that she was never to live in. She died far too soon in 1956. Howard and I continued to live on at Edgewater until the 1960s when the books seemed to have moved, all on their own, to Italy and so we moved with them until now; as I write, they are headed for California where I shall finally live in our fourth and final house, whose endless library seems to have been assembled by the sorcerer's apprentice.

My obsession with houses is the result of my mother's habit of marrying and divorcing. No sooner had she restored a house than she'd either leave a husband or he her. Since I was away in school or the army,

I never, as they say, settled in. So, eventually, I had to buy my own houses.

Howard and I lived at Edgewater for twenty years then sold it to a rich businessman who collected Greek Revival houses which he usually made museums out of and then gave to the public, enjoying no doubt a considerable tax deduction from a grateful nation. I've only set foot in the house once since the sale. It is now a sort of museum of nineteenth-century furniture.

I do dream about the house. In the dream I have somehow bought it back and I am about to move in. As I cross the tracks of the adjacent New York Central Railroad, I run into John Navins the postmaster of Barrytown who also kept a small general store in what had been the old Barrytown station house. Whenever we meet in this particular dream, he always says, "I knew you'd come back." But back to what? In the dream the lawn has vanished. The river is almost even with the columns. The island is large and stony. Inside the rooms are unfamiliar. And, of course, there is no one there. Plainly I, too, am a ghost as I wander through the empty rooms. Only old John Navins seems to be among the living. Yet in all his years beside the tracks he only took the train down to New York City once. Dutifully, he got off at Grand Central Terminal and walked out into the crowded street. He was so horrified by what he saw that he hurried back into the station and sat down in a waiting room where he remained until the next train took him back to Barrytown and his pre-ghostly existence. I've not seen him for several years now. Perhaps he's retired from haunting. To my distress Howard does not make many appearances in dreams other than the frustration ones where one cannot find the door to a flat. My father makes the odd appearance, as serene as ever. But I think of those as death dreams: he comes only at times when my own death is on my mind. Several times he has led me up a mountain to some wild landscape into which he disappears. Mercifully, I am spared visits from my mother. Sadly I never see the Gores anymore. My grandmother Dot had told me what horren-

Edgewater, the house I intended to live in to the end, with the spaniels Billy and Blanche. This is the autumn day when, after nearly twenty years, I sold the place and moved to Rome with the dogs. Howard had got there before me. Edgewater was built in 1820. The octagonal library is the work of A. J. Davis.

dous dreams she was having in her last days. The Senator did not tell me about his dreams but he'd answer questions that interested him. He was totally blind by his tenth year. So one of my first questions to him on the subject was: "Are you able to see again in your dreams?" He found that an interesting subject. The answer was, yes, he sometimes could. But as he pondered this "restored" vision he came to the conclusion that he could only see things which he had seen *before* the second accident blinded him. He could see green grass. Blue sky. But, no, he could not even imagine his wife or children or political colleagues. He sensed that they were present in certain dream-dramas but he had no faces to put to them. Voices? He thought that he must have heard voices in a light-less void. Could he visualize the color red? I was relentless but he was patient, even a bit curious. I learned that his father had taken him to a famous eye specialist in New Orleans when he was about twelve and the optic nerve in one eye (the other was missing) still registered light and dark and vague shadows but then all that faded away. Had he lived in our time he could have recovered a good deal of sight in at least the one eye. I recall a woman journalist telling him that, of course, there must be compensations. "There are none," was the hard response and he later referred to her as that Christian Scientist, not a compliment from some-one atheistically inclined who had survived a youth in religion-mad Mississippi. He liked to confront his more devout cousinage with con-tradictions in their Christian faith. Early in life his own family had split on religion. The Gores belonged to a long line of Methodist preachers but by the time of his father many of them were splitting off into Bap-tist groupings. His father, Thomas Madison Gore, the county clerk, be-came a Cambellite, an interesting sect of fundamentalists that wanted to prove every word of Gospel to be scientifically true. When my grandfa-ther was asked to which church he planned to go, he said, briskly, "I'm going to the Senate." He got through Lebanon Law School with the help of a cousin whose tuition his father had paid. Still an adolescent, he helped several adult members of his family to organize the Party of the People in Mississippi. He developed early as an orator and was known to contemporaries as Guv. In due course, he moved west to the Indian territories and helped organize Oklahoma as a state where he was elected their first senator in 1907 and served until 1937. His last years were spent working as an attorney for several Indian tribes that had been cheated of their land by the U.S. government. Not long after his death the tribes got a considerable settlement. There is a city named Gore in the state; he always threatened to go live there when its population was under a hundred but thought better of it when it became a city. I have never seen his house in Lawton if it still exists. It is somewhere near those ubiquitous railroad tracks on whose other side the future Joan Crawford was growing up at the same time as my mother, Nina, who was forbidden to play with her young contemporary because *her* mother was deemed a scarlet woman by the pious folk of the town.

THIRTY-EIGHT

———— ✳ ————

On October 3, 1975, I turned fifty, an event that I wanted to keep secret. I cannot imagine anyone willingly celebrating time's ruthless one-way passage. But that year friends decided to do something and Kathleen Tynan, second wife of the critic Kenneth Tynan, and my old friend Diana Phipps decided to give a party in London where over the years I had come to know more people than anywhere else. A club with a good cook was the site. Howard and I flew to London and stayed not as always before at the Connaught but at the Ritz. I remember I had a pile of letters to answer and so the morning of the third I was up early answering them in longhand. Then Howard and I took the lift down to the lobby. It was a small lift lined with mirrors. Halfway down it stopped to admit another passenger, a woman in a white trench coat. Our eyes met in mute shock: it was Jackie Kennedy Onassis. Relations between us had broken off after my row with Bobby in 1961 and time certainly had not improved my mood. First, the IRS went after my father with a long pointless audit. Then I heard from Mississippi that someone from

At the beach house of Kenneth and Kathleen Tynan and several of their children: Kathleen is at left, then director Tony Richardson, Princess Margaret, me, and Jack Nicholson. Ken was writing a biography of Laurence Olivier who, when he heard how much Ken was being paid for the book, ceased to cooperate and wrote his own tedious book. Ken, who was dying of emphysema, changed his publisher's contract to a sort of personal memoir; he died before he completed it. Then Kathleen, also dying of cancer, did finish the book. Each summer for several years she would come to La Rondinaia and faithfully do her exercises in the pool. Olivier, in explanation of his bad behavior, told me: "I owe Ken Tynan many things but not my life." My rejoinder was a muttered expletive. After all, it was Ken not Olivier who was most responsible for England's National Theatre.

Bobby's Justice Department had been snooping around trying to dig up scandal about Senator Gore while several court journalists were always available to think up items about me. I certainly never blamed Jackie for taking his side in a complicated unbecoming row but her contribution was that we had not known each other until a chance encounter at a horse show, the last place I would ever be found unless it was after dinner at the White House when Jackie dragged Jack and me there. With that in mind, to Howard's horror, I turned my back on her to discover in the mirror a smudge of ink on my brow. As I used a handkerchief to remove the ink the lift door opened and she sighed in her best Marilyn Monroe voice, "Bye-bye" and vanished into Piccadilly.

THIRTY-NINE

———— ✳ ————

Recently a new mystery was revealed. There is some TV footage of Jack, Jackie, and me making our entrance at a Washington horse show where I end up sitting to Jack's left; then there is Jackie to my left and an unknown lady behind us. Just visible, back of us, was the memorable hat of Alice Roosevelt Longworth who had been at dinner in what had once been her bedroom. A lady has currently written a book about life at the Kennedy court. I showed her the TV footage. She had questioned my story of the placement at the horse show. Apparently she had "proof" that Alice sat beside the president. I agreed that she should have but she didn't. The journalist then sent me an archival photograph of the event in which I have been neatly cropped out and replaced by Alice and her hat. Nowadays when we are more used to creative history and fictional presences this seems par for that particular course. But in *Palimpsest* there is a picture of Jack talking into my right ear at the horse show. This could not have happened unless I were sitting on poor Alice's lap, a most indecorous thing for me to have done. Later at my birthday party Princess Margaret provided me with extra dialogue in response to "Bye-bye."

Much of half a century of my English life was present at the birthday party. From the 1940s the novelist John Bowen. From the present day, Evangeline Bruce, wife to our ambassador, and then an ambassadress from long ago, Diana Cooper who spent her honeymoon with Duff Cooper at Villa Cimbrone back of our Ravello house. I have no list of who else was there. Diana Phipps who makes collages* out of pictures cut from newspapers and magazines did a fine memorial of the occasion including friends and foes as well as those present and absent. Clive James, a friend of Diana's, wrote an amiable poem to celebrate the occasion. Diana Cooper took it away to study at home. When I wrote her a polite note asking for it back she sent it to me along with my note requesting it, an odd bit of one-upmanship. As a child she had known and admired George Meredith, a friend of her mother. When he died she dressed herself in her mother's mourning clothes complete with thick veil, and attended Meredith's funeral where she was noticed by all as the mystery lady who sobbed so loudly throughout the service, adding unexpected romance to Meredith's troubled life.

Jackie had a good—even honest—response to publishers eager for her to write "the story of your life which has been so fascinating to so many people." "I know it has," she would say. "At least I know people say so but how can *I* write about it if I've forgotten it all?" But she had not forgotten that after the first bullet was fired at Dallas, Jack had said, "I've been hit." Since he wore a corset for his bad back all she needed to have done was pull him onto the car floor but she reacted too slowly in the shock of the moment. She was also bemused by the piece of his skull which she wanted to put back in place. The rest seems to have been confusion.

---

*Diana Phipps's collages (minus color) have been used as endpapers for this edition.

There was a small group of friends waiting at the airport in Washington. Angie Duke, chief of protocol, reported that her first words to him were, "Get me the plans for the funeral of Abraham Lincoln." Years later a friend asked her what she considered her greatest achievement. The answer was prompt: "That after all that I had gone through I did not go mad."

FORTY

———— ✳ ————

During the war years Princess Margaret was awed to meet an American giantess, Eleanor Roosevelt. At six foot she was, literally, to the small Hanoverian, a giantess. Eleanor was a permanent ambassador for the president, making her reports, giving advice that was not always welcome to that consummate games player. Princess Margaret (PM for short) had an eye for detail and an ear, too, if, for nothing else, absurdity. The great family figure of her childhood was Uncle David, briefly King Edward VIII, thereafter, lengthily, aka Duke of Windsor. Neither he nor "the woman he loved" was welcome in England. Although PM and her sister, Queen Elizabeth II, were curious to meet this crown-crossed couple their mother saw to it that no such occasion would arise. "It's all a woman's show now," said the Duchess of Windsor to me, bitter that her husband had been given no proper work to do other than the governorship of some Caribbean islands. Finally Uncle David died and his remains were brought back to be interred: only then did the Queen Mother relent and allow the Duchess to attend the funeral.

While the family was duly assembled, PM reports that "Lilibet and I were so fascinated to see and hear this legendary figure in the flesh that we stationed ourselves at either end of the sofa where, side by side, Mummy and the Duchess sat, at peace at last, or so it seemed. I am rather good at eavesdropping, my sister not. So I heard more of what was said. The Duchess was a well-preserved old lady from the 1930s. The first thing that she said to Mummy was, 'Do you have an upstairs or a downstairs kitchen?' Mummy looked a bit alarmed. Not only does she not know *where* the food comes from, she only knows that it is on the table three times a day. Luckily, the Duchess was quite prepared to fill any gaps in the conversation: 'We tried both and I prefer the upstairs as there is so much less moving about. Naturally, it depends upon how many guests you are entertaining.' At this point they were interrupted." The family was to assemble for the funeral service. The Duchess remained behind and watched from a window. After the service, the Queen Mother returned to the sofa, radiating charm and condolences to the family's ancient enemy. PM again took up her place at the listening post only to hear the Duchess ask, yet again: "Do you have an upstairs or a downstairs kitchen?" Not long after when PM was in New York she got orders from the palace to pay a call on the Duchess. She was greeted at the door by several yapping dogs and Wallis Windsor. As PM dutifully patted the dogs she said, "Now I know the reason why you come so seldom to England." "Well," said Wallis, "they are *one* of the reasons."

PM spoke of the royal family with expectable reverence not unmixed with humor and the occasional surrealist note: "The Queen is uncommonly talented in ways that you might not suspect," she proclaimed. Suspecting nothing, I asked, "In what way?" "Well, she can put on a *very* heavy tiara while hurrying down a flight of stairs *with no mirror*."

One bright hot summer PM organized a house party at the Royal Lodge near Windsor. "You can easily recognize it. It is *very* pink." And so it was, set among tall trees. The lodge had been built by the Prince

Regent whose portrait by Lawrence scowled peevishly at us in the terrace sitting room. I was assigned to what I think was called the blue bedroom. There were three or four other houseguests and PM had got King George's cook out of retirement for the weekend. The Queen Mother who often lived at the lodge had retreated from the unusual heat to Scotland. We swam in an ancient pool full of drowning bees.

On the seventy-fifth birthday of Jack Heinz his wife, Drue, gave a grand evening party at Ascot where they had rented a house. There was a tent with an orchestra for dancing. Another tent for those invited to dinner. A Ferris wheel. A pond. Swans.

I should note that no one is supposed to attend an event after the Queen's arrival but PM and I, at the lodge, lingered over gin and tonics. On the lawn of the Heinzes' house the Queen frowned at her sister, who said within my hearing, "How's it going?" The Queen replied: "We have shaken many hands," which meant many Americans were on hand; the sovereign is not supposed to be touched by subjects: males incline their heads as in a bow, females curtsey. PM presented me, I did the nod. The Queen said: "You are staying at the lodge. Which room?" I said I thought it was called the blue bedroom. Suddenly the Queen's girlish voice was replaced by the voice of Lady Bracknell: "*My room!*" she boomed. Then she fled across the lawn.

At dinner I sat next to PM. Across from her was Senator John Heinz, Jack's son, soon to be killed in a plane crash. "Isn't he beautiful," PM muttered to me. I complimented her on her taste. As dinner ended, after-dinner guests poked their heads through the tent flaps: the first head belonged to Rex Harrison. When, finally, the Queen rose I ended up on the lawn where Rex, querulous as always, said, "Who was that awful-looking man sitting next to the Queen?" I said he was in charge of the Heinz interests in Ireland and so he was the largest single employer in an island that was not to become prosperous until the premiership of Charlie Haughey.

After the dancing was done we returned to the lodge where PM gave us a reading from a book of mine called *Duluth*. Some of the descriptions were very graphic but the several young men who had come back to the lodge with the house party were, happily, clueless. As PM shut the book, she said, "I don't know what there is in me that is so low and base, that I love this book." I can answer that now that years and death have separated us: she was far too intelligent for her station in life. She often had a bad press, the usual fate of wits in a literal society. "Also," she said, "it was inevitable: when there are two sisters and one is the Queen who must be the source of honor and all that is good while the other must be the focus of the most creative malice, the evil sister." She was stoic; nothing to be done but one can note her kindness to friends, to those employees whose pensions she paid out of fairly meager resources, not to mention her steadfast loyalty to a system that never in the end did as much for her as she sacrificed for it.

FORTY-ONE

———————— ✳ ————————

Someone has dug up some irritable letters of mine to various publications. Apparently in the British *New Statesman* (August 28, 1976) I took exception to A. J. P. Taylor's obituary of my old friend Tom Driberg. Tom had been chairman of the Labour Party as well as member of Parliament for years. He was the original William Hickey, a sort of highbrow columnist (yes, there was once such a thing and in a Beaverbrook newspaper, too). He was a dedicated Christian as well as Marxist and a powerful debater particularly on television. That he is not easily summed up is a tribute to his originality. He enjoyed writing about the higher Bohemia and championed the Sitwells when it was not fashionable; then he continued to do so, most bravely, when it was. A formidable gossip, his world of glamorous ladies overlapped with Waugh's to the delight of neither. He was on his way to the airport to go to Ravello when he died in a taxicab. He had been at work on his memoirs written in a perfect hand on special cards. Compton Mackenzie had written a roman à clef about him called *Thin Ice* which just about says it all. When the Labour

Party was holding its conference in Scotland, I think it was toward the end of the war, Tom was arrested while having carnal knowledge of a Norwegian sailor. Happily for Tom the arresting officer was a Labour voter and, best of all, a fan of Tom's Hickey column. Tom applied the extreme unction of his hortatory style to the policeman about how this brave blameless lad, who had been fighting with the Allies against Hitler, knew no English; had just happened to be in port and should be allowed to return to his ship. The policeman told the brave lad to return to the war. The lad fled. As Tom told me the story, with some satisfaction, he noted that without the sailor's presence there was no case against him. He then proceeded to charm the policeman. They discussed politics. Then over the years Tom became a friend of both the policeman and his wife who sent Tom the policeman's library when he died.

The historian A. J. P. Taylor's obituary of Tom in the *New Statesman*, a paper I wrote for in those days, inspired me to respond to his condescension and inaccuracies. Particularly this observation: "Tom was also homosexual and flagrant and unashamed." This was a bit much even by the lower-middle-class insular standards of that day. I wrote that "I was not aware that homosexuality was something to be ashamed of. Certainly Taylor would not write of Lloyd George that he was heterosexual, flagrant and unashamed. I daresay Taylor meant compulsive or promiscuous; even so, shame hardly enters in." Then Taylor warms to his subject: "Tom was not at all a clever man or an intellectual. He did not understand either Marx or Keynes." This is a startling non sequitur. First, Tom knew as much Marx and Keynes as was good for him; second, a close knowledge of outdated economic theory is not a decisive factor in determining whether or not a man is an intellectual. Tom's knowledge of poetry was vast; his mind was literary; it was also divergent not convergent. He was often an inspired theologian; he had a formidable gift for logic (without which it is hardly possible to be an intellectual), his ear for the false note in poetry or reasoning was near-perfect. As for not being "clever" . . . Well, I have no idea what Taylor means by cleverness. Admittedly, Tom never taught school.

On July 7, 1977, I wrote to *The New York Times*:

In what looks to be a review of my new collection of essays [*Matters of Fact and of Fiction*], your dispenser of book-chat tells us that my attack on nearly two hundred years of American imperialism as symbolized by the U.S. Military Academy at West Point (where my father was an instructor when I was born) is the result of an "unresolved hostility toward his father, further evidence of which, some would argue, is Mr. Vidal's cheerfully admitted homosexuality."

This is quintessential *New York Times* reporting. First, it is ill-written, hence ill-edited. Second, it is inaccurate. Third, it is unintelligent in the vulgar Freudian way. There is no evidence of an "unresolved hostility" toward my father in the pages under review or elsewhere in my work. Quite the contrary. I quote from *Two Sisters, a Novel in the form of a Memoir*: "my father was the only man I ever entirely liked. . . ." Nowhere in my writing have I "admitted" ("cheerfully" or dolefully) to homosexuality, or to heterosexuality. Even the dullest of mental therapists no longer accepts the proposition that cold-father-plus-clinging-mother-equals-fag-offspring.

These demurs to one side, I am grateful to your employee for so beautifully demonstrating in a single sentence so many of the reasons why *The New York Times* is a perennially bad newspaper and bound to champion the disreputable likes of Judith Miller [name added later, obviously].

FORTY-TWO

———— ✳ ————

I suspect that I have just celebrated my last Ferragosto in Italy. It is an amiable holiday in August celebrating the birth of our great emperor Augustus who gave the world the Pax Romana, a long period of peace and prosperity after a chaotic time of wars, civil and otherwise. I cannot imagine any of our recent presidents being remembered for so long much less praised generation after generation. But last night was his night and we watched the fireworks as reflected in the bay of Salerno. All the while preparing the books to be moved back to the U.S., a melancholy business at best. For some reason I keep thinking of Nureyev who came to say good-bye some ten years ago. He had been putting in order his house on an island opposite Positano up the coast from us. "From bedroom I can see, on the right, sun come up and, on the left, sun go down. I die there. Is perfect." He had AIDS. But at regular intervals a doctor from Paris would arrive and change his blood. When this happened, he would be full of energy for a few weeks. On the island, next to his house, was a studio built by a previous occupant, Massine the dancer-choreographer. Revived by new blood Rudi would switch on a gramophone in the studio and dance. The upper part of his body had begun to dwindle away but the legs were unchanged. He sweated like a horse. Finally, Rudi came to lunch with us. As usual, he threw off all his clothes and plunged into the pool. "Must go back to America, doctor says." After lunch and a great deal of white wine he lay down on the sofa in my study. I switched on the television: it was during a time of dramatic transition in Moscow. We watched as the statue of a chief of the KGB was pulled down. Only the bronze boots remained vertical. "They make good quality boots back then," Rudi observed; and slept. He expressed few political opinions on Russian matters. He hated it when the press depicted him as a defector from Communism. "I get out only to dance more. Is frozen there, the great dance companies. So I left."

I never heard him denounce the Soviet system. On the other hand, he was no enthusiast for our system. He was particularly irritated when he was criticized for not admitting that he had AIDS. "If I do, I cannot reenter U.S. Law says no one with such a disease can be allowed in. So I must be silent." He had a great deal of property in and around Washington, D.C., where he had installed relatives. He was also eager to get his mother to America if only for a visit. The Soviet authorities were cooperative but the Americans were not. Someone suggested that he appeal to President Carter. This proved to be a disaster. The beloved ex-president-to-be was not yet on view. Instead, "wreathed in malaise" as he called it, he was in no mood to grant favors to someone like Nureyev. Rudi was still in a rage as he described Carter's treatment of him. He had been summoned to the White House where Carter reminded him that the leader of the free world had quite a lot on his plate and had no time to bother about the mother of a famous dancer. Rudi was shocked by the little man's bad manners. It was all so like Rudi's native Siberia where "criminals" were sent and petty bureaucrats ruled. Carter made it very clear that he would do nothing to help Rudi's mother to visit America. Rudi's volatile Mongol temperament was

Nureyev pays a final call at La Rondinaia.

aroused: "I expected better from an American president so I cursed him."

"You did what?" I was not certain I'd understood him. He was grinning in memory. "I cursed him first in Russian but there was no translator so I cursed him again in English." When I asked for some technical details of the curse—bell, book, and candle, say? "I told this Carter he would be punished for not allowing an old woman to come visit her son, for his cruelty and his rudeness and then I said that because of this behavior he would lose the coming election, which he did and *all* thanks to my curse. Very powerful, these Russian curses." I told Rudi he should open an office for people who could use his supernatural powers: today, of course, he would be overworked. Then I walked him to the gate of La Rondinaia and, no doubt affected by this talk of curses, I imitated an old Russian friend and made the sign of the cross on his chest: he bowed gravely. He died soon after. Someone who knew him far better than I said it was like a powerful flame going out.

In early 1978 Howard and I bought a house in the Hollywood Hills. The Red Brigades in Italy had kidnapped then murdered the former prime minister Aldo Moro and everyone's advice was "get out of Italy which is falling into chaos." Since chaos is the normal state of that oddly happy nation or perhaps I should say entity I did not fear the apparently rising tide of Communism all over the world possibly because I knew so many interested political and media types in Washington whose wild allegations could then be checked by consulting certain wise Italians or, indeed, Europeans of any sort grown sick of our constant howling wolf when, more and more, we were being identified as *the* wolf advancing upon the house of the three little pigs. When asked what advantage there is to having two houses, one in the Hollywood Hills and the other on the Amalfi coast, I have seldom had an answer. But now, after half a century, I am aware of receiving a wider range of information about what is going on in the world as opposed to the non-news and propaganda of most of our media. Certainly the Italian Communist Party so often demonized by our media was never of any great danger to anyone while radical splinter groups like the Red Brigades could hardly be called Communist: Moro was killed because he favored what Italians call "the historic compromise" between the conservative Christian Democrats and the mildly liberal Communists, each anathema to certain incoherent American activists of the sixties. Had we not intervened so ferociously in the election of 1948 the compromise would have taken place earlier to, one suspects, no great effect, good or bad.

FORTY-THREE

──────── ✳ ────────

I used to see Moro at the Quirinale palace on the national day of the republic. He was a weary sort of realist with, as someone wrote, "a thousand years of sirocco in his eyes." He had developed a prose style of total opaqueness. When Luigi Barzini once asked him why, as prime minister, he spoke so cryptically Moro said, "If I spoke clearly about our situation everyone would emigrate."

Barzini was a witty journalist, son of another famous journalist. During fascism he fell afoul of Mussolini who sent him into "home exile" in the south of Italy; specifically, to Amalfi. Luigi's wife, a Feltrinelli with money, envisaged a hovel with no running water and so she shipped an entire bathroom of white marble to Amalfi where, like some sinister sculpture, toilet, bathtub, and lonely bidet ended up on the Amalfi beach for many years while the Barzinis enjoyed their exile at a local hotel.

Howard and I bought the house in Los Angeles not to flee the Red Brigades but to prepare for the hospital years which came even sooner than either suspected. Meanwhile we stayed on in Ravello except when work or politics brought me back.

Early 1978 while I was having dinner in Washington with my half sister our mother died in New York, of cancer. I'd not seen her in years but I did read her attack on me in *Time* magazine printed under the headline "A Mother's Love." But I had other things than "love" on my mind.

April 5, 1978, I spoke at Arlington Street Church in Boston on behalf of the Boston-Boise Committee. A witch hunt of Salemesque intensity was under way in Boston. Twenty-four men had been arrested at Revere Beach for consorting with local youths (of whom not one was a child): apparently some of the youths rented their favors. During that summer the local police were "cracking down on same-sexualists" at the beach, in the libraries, though not yet in the Irish Catholic Church. Civil libertarians, in order to ensure fair trials for those who had been cracked down upon, formed a group called the National Jury Project to determine whether or not fair trials were possible in so heated an atmosphere to which additional heat would presently be added by the arrival in town of that scourge of Sodom, singer Anita Bryant. Out of the blue, the Boston-Boise group asked me to speak at the church in order to raise money not so much for the defense of the Revere Beachers as to draw attention to the local all-out war on those deemed "homosexual." Only now, reading old correspondence, am I beginning to grasp why 1,500 people crowded the church to hear me. Unfortunately, I was confronted with every speaker's nightmare: I had no written text; worse, no close knowledge of the events leading up to my appearance. I was dull. After the speech I was introduced to some members of the Boston-Boise Committee. Boise, Idaho, had recently endured a similar witch hunt where most of the male civic leaders of that city were charged with engaging in sexual acts with willing ephebes. John Gerassi, author of *The Boys of Boise*, a book that shocked the nation largely because, as was noted at the time, "the guilty parties were all married men with children and grandchildren," just like the Revere Beachers who were mostly married blue-collar men. At the back of the church an amiable scholarly figure asked me to autograph his copy of *Burr*. I duly wrote his name, "Robert M. Bonin," little suspecting how soon our names would be juxtaposed in the Boston press. When I signed that book for Mr. Bonin I had no idea that he was the chief justice of Massachusetts. A week later he was being vilified in the Boston press for having come to hear me speak at a fund-raiser for twenty-four sex criminals, (*sic*) et cetera . . .

I promptly wrote Judge Bonin to say how sorry I was to have been used as a pretext to destroy a much-admired jurist. Bonin responded graciously: "I had made other misjudgments but none so rash as underestimating the extensive and intensive aspects of homophobia and anti-Semitism. Massachusetts has its own home-grown and flourishing Generals Brown and Anita Bryants." Judge Bonin, as a Jew, did not suit the prejudices of the Roman Catholic–WASP judiciary of his state. Bonin's subsequent letter of resignation to Governor Michael S. Dukakis is balanced and dignified. "The Legislature has spoken. The approval of the Address was unjust and is a bad precedent. Address, without required reasons and trial is a dreadful procedure lacking in due process. I hope it will not be a prologue to future actions against other judges. I cannot conceive of Address for the impropriety of 'neglectful' attendance at a lecture." ("Neglectful" is a weird word to use for hearing a speech in a church.) He also remarks that he had been pre-tried in the media. He quotes Solzhenitsyn: "The press has become the greatest power within the Western countries, more powerful than the legislature, the executive, and the judiciary . . . hastiness and superficiality are the psychic disease of the twentieth century and more than anywhere else is this disease reflected in the press." And so he went, most cheerfully, on his way. It is a wonder that he could have endured such an establishment for as long as he did. Meanwhile, I started to write more and more about contemporary politics.

FORTY-FOUR

---- ✳ ----

A few years ago the BBC wondered if I would do a program on the American South and its families. Incidentally it is only British television that wants to do interesting projects on our native land: with few exceptions, the home team deals only in entertainers if, of course, they can be guaranteed not to entertain. Someone had noticed that although the WASPs are in themselves a small minority in the South they compensate for their fewness in numbers by their webs of cousinage in families which go back to the 1600s like my grandmother Gore, a Kay from South Carolina whose family had emigrated from Bury in Lancashire in the eighteenth century. Since there were so few British settlers in the Southern states there was not much of anyone for these immigrants to marry so they kept marrying into the same families. I have never been able to remember what relation I am to Albert Gore Junior even though his father, a Tennessee senator, once explained it to me on television in San Francisco (no, I don't recall what he said but he did say that had I been elected to Congress in 1960 "our relationship would have been much closer," which perhaps says it all).

Once a year the Gores hold a family reunion in northern Mississippi which I eventually attended in the interest of a documentary on me rather than on that white Anglo-Saxon enclave in the Southern states, a project abandoned because the BBC did not want to get involved in the business of race or, as my grandmother Gore liked to say, if any descendant of mine should marry someone colored I'll come back and haunt 'em. When I was grown I liked to tease her with the knowledge that our blood had been commingled with that of the other race ever since the country began; she would then simply change the subject and complain about how the Civil War was the vengeance of God on a generation of Southern boys who preferred shooting and hunting to going to school. The producers had also been put off by Jimmy Carter himself who had thought the program was to be about me when the subject was about kin and all of us. I had of course sent him a telegram after his disastrous intervention with helicopters in Iran during the hostage crisis, reminding him that honor required his resignation for having disgraced the country. Had he perhaps taken my censure amiss?

Finally, he and I do share a most distinguished ancestor, John Kay of Bury (1733–1764). According to the *Dictionary of National Biography*, "Kay's improvements in machinery for weaving continue in use to the present day" (the Flying Shuttle). He was the founder of the first great improvements in the manufacture of cloth by which employment is now given to hundreds of thousands of people while in 1760 his son Robert invented the shuttle drop box. I fear that neither Jimmy nor I have ever lived up to our brilliant heritage.

FORTY-FIVE

—————— ✳ ——————

As I now pack up the books and pictures that Howard and I acquired at La Rondinaia since we moved in thirty-three years ago I keep thinking of my one conversation with John Steinbeck at a friend's apartment in Manhattan. We were both talking about houses and the urge to put down roots "for good." I'd just got Edgewater on the Hudson. I could not imagine wanting to live anyplace else. Yes, summers were too hot and winters too cold but it was a perfect house in so many ways. I suspect that it really was what I'd always wanted and that is why I still dream that I have somehow got it back and am moving back in again and, of course, Howard is still alive. Steinbeck was of the same mind. He said, "How many times I've settled somewhere *for good* and never wanted to leave until the inevitable day comes when I move on and the place is emptying out and we are suddenly all gone and living in a new place." As I write this, I am getting ready to move on and a third of my life is being packed up and I am again transient—neither here nor there.

Here I am packing up some pictures and 8,000 books, the end of an era for me on the Amalfi coast, ready to face the future in the Hollywood Hills with a new knee made of titanium.

These rehearsals for death take more and more out of one until at the end there is, I suspect, nothing at all left except Howard's old dressing gown hanging on the back of his bathroom door, a refuge for moths, which Rita maintains are fireflies on the ground that I could not know the difference.

FORTY-SIX

––––––––––––––––– ✳ –––––––––––––––––

A television crew has come and gone. There is to be a program on Italo Calvino, the first in Italy. So we go into the *salone* and eerily the camera is set up on the exact spot where he and his wife, Chichita, sat at dinner on the day that I was made an honorary citizen of Ravello. There had been music in the piazza. From Rome had come the Calvinos, Luigi Barzini, the critic Alberto Arbasino. Speeches were made. Barzini nicely compared me to Marion Crawford, an American novelist who had lived up the coast at Sorrento and whose house by the sea had been envied by Henry James who did not in the least envy Crawford's worldly novels. A year or so later I was to preside over the transformation of the Crawford villa into a museum by zealous admirers from the University of Naples. Each Italian village seems to have a tutelary foreign writer in place. Capri is celebrated for Norman Douglas whose family, though from Scotland, had lived in the mountains above Feldkirch while he himself was associated with the Amalfi coast or Siren Land as he called it and, finally, Capri. I had a number of occasions to meet the old man who was supported by an admirer, Kenneth Macpherson; then one day they were all gone. Graham Greene lived at Annacapri on the top of the hill. Occasionally he would ring me and I'd ask him to stay in Ravello on his way to his Capri house but he would always become oddly coy: "You see I am traveling with an old friend to whom I am not married and there are those who object to this sort of irregular relationship." I told him that I was not an objector but we never saw him in Ravello nor he us on Capri. But he and I saw a great deal of each other in Moscow when Gorbachev held an antinuclear meeting in the Kremlin for well-wishers of his glasnost and perestroika. Graham spoke for culture, a perfect fifteen-minute speech without a note. When, admiringly, I remarked on this to Norman Mailer, he said, "Every Englishman can talk for fifteen minutes on any subject without a note." It was on this trip that Greene got to see the spy Philby again and came to the conclusion that not only was Gorbachev going to rid us of the cold war but that only the KGB, from which he came, was sufficiently educated and competent to govern the post-Soviet nation. All in all, Graham proved a fairly competent prophet. In those days he lived in the south of France where he was quietly feuding with an old friend of mine, Anthony Burgess, who had made the mistake of describing Graham's conversation while drinking. Graham had many tall tales to tell but he disliked seeing them later in print. I defended Anthony, warily. Graham was suddenly accusing: "But *you* like to go on television and I don't." I said I liked to talk publicly about politics, and street corners were no longer desirable venues. "Burgess," he said, "is on television all the time in France." "What," I asked, "does he talk about?" Graham scowled and whispered, "His *books*." I agreed that *this* was insufferable. "I never do television," said Graham, "and, as you see, if I can help it, I never let them photograph me." Since our arrival at the Kremlin Graham had been constantly televised and photographed which I reminded him of. "Ah," he said cryptically, "this is the east and those things don't matter here." Whether or not they did, he was hugely popular with the east Europeans at the conference where he was a Burgess-like presence. He was particularly exciting on the subject of Castro with whom he had fought side by side in Oriente Province during the revolution. I could not tell if he was making it up as he went along or whether or not he was actually calling upon memory. His eyes were curiously glazed, like mica.

FORTY-SEVEN

———————— ✳ ————————

Opposite my desk as I write, two pieces of parchment testify that I am an honorary citizen of Ravello as well as of Los Angeles, and my favorite award: a hammered silver plaque from the cities of Magna Graecia for *Creation* and my contribution to the classical world. I think the award was presented in Crotone where Pythagoras died. Certainly his cult still haunts the coast which I shall soon be leaving for a more satisfactory world. Yet again.

As I look about my study I see a row of books bound in dark blue leather. Something annoys me. I open Montaigne's essays in the Screech translation. The source of annoyance is there. But where? Why? The book falls open, automatically, at his essay on Lying which I often reread when faced with the excess of lies in our public life.

Lying is an accursed vice. It is only our words which bind us together and make us human. If we realized the horror and weight of lying we would see that it is more worthy of the stake than other crimes. I find that people normally waste time quite inappropriately punishing children for innocent misdemeanours, tormenting them for thoughtless actions which lead nowhere and leave no trace. It seems to me that the only faults which we should vigorously attack as soon as they arise and start to develop are lying and, a little below that, stubbornness. Those faults grow up with the children. Once let the tongue acquire the habit of lying and it is astonishing how impossible it is to make it give it up . . . If a lie, like truth, had only one face we could be on better terms, for certainty would be the reverse of what the liar said. But the reverse side of truth has a hundred thousand shapes and no defined limits. The Pythagoreans make good to be definite and finite; evil they make indefinite and infinite.

A clumsy journalist at *Time* magazine some years ago did a cover story on me which was odd. It was at the time of Nixon's fall and since the piece was about my novel *1876* and some of the not always sterling truths that our founders were capable of, the essay on me was entitled "The Sins of the Fathers," a standard propagandist erasure of news the publisher does not want taken too seriously: sometimes known as "they all do it," so what's the fuss? Currently, to counteract all the talk of stolen elections in 2000 and 2004 a dozen journalists now assure us that our elections have always been corrupt; which is hardly true. Recently the same *Time* magazine journalist felt it was time that I be discredited as vain and self-absorbed. So he wrote as if he had actually been inside my study which he hasn't and saw hundreds of blue leather-bound books all by me. But they are mostly worn leather-bound reference books of the sort I doubt that this kind of journalist consults. But then more than ever in my lifetime the great whopping lie is seriously in vogue.

FORTY-EIGHT

———— ✳ ————

In a fit of absentmindedness I said that I would serve as president of the jury of the Venice Film Festival in 1990. I usually avoid festivals, prize-givings, and every sort of bureaucratic event involving the arts. I can't think why I said yes. There would be, I was told—warned (?)—a feminist jury. Why not? I thought. I had broken a lance or two in the gender wars on the side of the ladies. Finally, it is unwise to forgo a trip to Venice at almost any time. So Howard and I were booked into a hotel on the Lido. By and large, I have never had much to do with the media that concerns itself with cinema. The journalists involved are often off-duty screenwriters and their world in Italy is somewhat Byzantine and inbred. I thought I'd have nothing more to do than see a dozen or two films and vote with the other jurors for best director, et cetera. But I soon realized it was not going to be that easy. I'd been reading a book by or about Cocteau describing his miserable time as president of that Cannes Film Festival where I'd won the Critics' Prize for *The Best Man* in 1964. I recalled Jacob, the president of the Cannes Festival, as an intelligent charming figure and was delighted that he was going to serve on my jury. Also on the jury were Omar Sharif and three or four ladies from Scandinavia and Russia. I'd known Omar from my time as screenwriter on *The Night of the Generals*, the second film I did with Sam Spiegel. Everyone asked why I did a *second* film since with Spiegel there was always trouble about payment or credit or both. My cheerful response was, "I couldn't believe it the first time." Also, I had grown morbidly fond of Sam with his vast appetite for food and hookers. Gadge Kazan's wife complained that she found Sam very conventional when it came to scripts and I said he was so conventional that he was classic. He also belonged to the old school of the Producer is god and only He can contribute meaningfully to the script. But Sam had changed; since a series of great successes, all publicity must now be about him: he was being presented to the public as the new Sam Goldwyn. He was also more than ever abrasive with his directors. He liked to pick first-rate directors whose careers were not doing well. He had also cannily signed up Peter O'Toole and Omar Sharif for a second film each after *Lawrence of Arabia*. I do not believe that I am revealing confidences when I say that each resented being paid minimal salaries.

On the Venice jury Omar charmed the ladies and I felt that we would have a comfortable gondola ride to the various Lion prizes. Unfortunately, Omar overdid the charm. The ladies, plus Omar, were a majority of the jury: this meant that practically every prize would go to a different lady: few men were to be winners. Since the best director at Venice that season was Martin Scorsese with his latest film *Goodfellas* it never occurred to me that anyone else would be chosen, with the possible exception of Tom Stoppard who had directed his own *Rosencrantz & Guildenstern Are Dead*. But Omar's dread charm had swept all the ladies before it. As a sign of solidarity he voted along with his Scandinavian harem. On the first ballot a truly awful film by a Danish woman called *Sirup* (the movie not the lady) won for best screenplay. The managerial head of the jury for the festival looked ill. The brilliant Jacob, if nothing else, must have seen the primacy of his festival at Cannes as-

Claire Luce and I at a ball in Venice in 1961, years before my jury duty. We are in what was Robert Browning's study. Each has just misquoted him.

sured for at least another decade. But not for nothing had I been Tammany Hall's choice as delegate for the 1960 Democratic convention, instructed to vote for Kennedy. I made a Bushesque speech in favor of total democracy which meant that best picture and director be voted for *jointly* to prevent overlapping prizes. The lady from Moscow gave me a weary look: she had met my sort before in the Soviet paradise. Meanwhile I had a word with Omar who was now as one with the party line. A Swedish lady spluttered but by then I was busy awarding best actress to *her* choice while the auteur of *Sirup* got best screenplay award. The ladies were reasonably pleased. I waited until the end for best film award. In a voice of sweet reason I said, "We are supposed to award these prizes to the best in each category. Since a number of ladies are angry that we have celebrated yet again gratuitous masculine violence, which we all deplore, by giving Scorsese the best director award which he deserves for at least half a dozen other films I think that we should break with tradition and give the Gold Lion to what, after all, is the best film in competition: *Rosencrantz & Guildenstern Are Dead* by Tom Stoppard." A pair of journalists on the jury had been leaking our proceedings to the world press and they promptly sent up black-and-white smoke signals. But we now had a Pope—Stoppard—teeth all around me were grinding. I was told that Olivier's *Hamlet* had been booed by the Italian press. They also disliked Shakespeare. Later, when I went out onstage to announce the winners, I was loudly booed but not before I murmured, "At least, for once, the best film got the best prize." Later I read that the producers who had released the film had once released one of mine and that I'd been paid off. Italy! Thus, on a high note, I ended my jury duty. For good.

FORTY-NINE

———— ✳ ————

"When did you fall out with Tennessee?" is a question that the odd specialist in such arcana asks me, to which there is no answer. "When did you fall in?" might be more to the point. But I am now navigating several volumes of his letters and conversations with him and it is a dizzying experience. What I used to call his night-blooming paranoia is often on display and strange stories crop up in the oddest places. The strangest concerned the first novel of Paul Bowles, *The Sheltering Sky*, which I had got to John Lehmann in England when a publisher declined it because "it was not a novel." In the forties there were many people who regarded themselves as specialists in what was and what was not. I recall a concert of Bowles' where one critic complained that the music was not music and Paul responded by explaining that the score and the instruments combined proved that it could not be anything other than music by any standard. The Bird wanted to be helpful to *The Sheltering Sky* so he asked *The New York Times* to let him review it. They did. Then there was some mix-up about getting the proofs to the Bird which he immediately surmised was a rejection of his review which began with a cheery assault on Truman Capote and me whose "frisky antics" though "precociously knowing and singularly charming" (doubly would have been a more telling adverb) could not be counted on "for those gifts that arrive by no other way than the experience and contemplation of a truly adult mind." When galleys of this review did not arrive the Bird assumed that I had used my great influence at *The New York Times* to suppress his review entirely. He was not one to pay much attention to the sad tales of others. If he had, he would have known that I had no influence in this quarter. Later he writes Donald Windham that he had done me an injustice. But there was worse to come. He greatly admired one of Windham's novels. He had also read the manuscript of a novel that I have never published. He even sent it on to Jay Laughlin at New Directions as my best work. Then his paranoia like a great branch of bougainvillea starts blossoming. Apparently, the manuscript of mine bears a suspicious resemblance to Windham's novel. Another great flower unfolds. Windham wonders how I could have read it since it was not yet published? A riot of blooms. Apparently I was in his literary agent's office where I found a carbon copy which I either copied then and there or memorized on the spot in order to plagiarize at my leisure. Windham, somewhat deficient in humor, reports in his notes to the Williams-Windham correspondence that he was, for this publication, obliged to read my early novels and found no trace of himself in those inimitable works. The thought of me sitting in a literary agent's office looking for texts to plunder shows how close to madness these two troubled friends had sailed. I was also aware that in his letters the Bird always tried to please the recipient and because Windham had a "bitchy" side the Bird would decorate his text with unpleasant tales about friends and foes, calculated to give pleasure. In one of the letters the Bird notes that "I got five sets of notices on the Arthur Miller play *Death of a Salesman*. Five different people sent them. It is hard to analyze one's feelings about the triumphs of another artist. There is likely to be a touch of the invidious in your feelings which makes you feel cheap and shameful. I liked the play when I read it, but I must say the great success of it is a surprise . . . I think Gadge must deserve more credit than the notices give him." In a letter to our friend Maria St. Just the Bird writes in 1960, rather sadly, apropos the success of my play *The Best Man*: "It looks as if this is Gore's year." But despite masses of bougainvillea over the years we usually got on largely because the same things—and people—made us laugh. On the other hand, his queenly entourage really got on my nerves. But with time they defected and there we were occupying at times the same midsummer night's dream. Fairies away! as proud Titania once yelled.

I began this memoir in Los Angeles on the last day of 2004. Now it is September 2005 and I am in Ravello, Italy, with no telephone, the result of a series of storms due to global warming: the principal fact of our lives even though, as they say in Washington, the jury is still out on whether or not such a thing is taking place. Meanwhile television is still working and we can observe the catastrophe that has left most of New Orleans under water. The Italians are astonished at the casualness with which the American government goes about saving those clinging to life atop the roofs of buildings. Tact keeps the local press from noting what every American knows: those who have been abandoned by lifesavers belong to our permanent underclass: the African Americans. The failures of the administration to save lives in the drowned city is further proof that any first-world militarized nation can easily defeat the United States in a modern war. We are not set up to survive a serious attack. Excuses fill the establishment press. Because of our altruistic leadership states like Louisiana and Mississippi have sent their National Guardsmen abroad to bring freedom and democracy to two countries that we were obliged to smash to bits so that they might one day enjoy true freedom, et cetera. Now the changed climate is doing to us what we did to Iraq and Afghanistan and are planning to do to Iran and other oil producers.

FIFTY

———————— ✳ ————————

Labor Day has come and gone along with New Orleans where I spent that long-ago winter when I did not go to Ceylon. Labor Day 1950 was when Howard and I met but since I have never understood when Labor Day itself is apt to be proclaimed I'd forgot our anniversary until the last one a few weeks before he died. He was pleasantly surprised. We had been together fifty-three years. He confessed that he thought he was just passing through my life and was surprised as the decades began to stack up and we were still together. But then it is easy to sustain a relationship when sex plays no part and impossible, I have observed, when it does. Each had a sex life apart from the other: all else including our sovereign, Time, was shared. I've just been reading a book of conversations with the Bird whom I used to see at Memorial Hospital visiting Frank Merlo who was dying of lung cancer. On a less perilous floor Howard was having a benign tumor of the thyroid removed. The Bird was very much school of Elizabeth Barrett Browning: I shall but love thee better after death. That is the romantic disposition. He forgot at the end that he and

Frank had been separated for some time before his death. The final row had involved Frank throwing a roast leg of lamb at the Bird who had providentially ducked.

I note that I began this memoir with a natural disaster, the earthquakes and tsunami in Southeast Asia, and now I draw to a conclusion with the catastrophe in the Gulf of Mexico where a racist ruling class abandoned the African American inhabitants of the Gulf and did not do so well either by whites without money. Money is now a Great Wall of China separating American rich from poor, a division that is beginning to seem as eternal as the Great Wall itself.

FIFTY-ONE

———— ✳ ————

On my table there is a copy of *Gore Vidal's America*, by Dennis Altman. I am writing this commentary on my eightieth birthday which Howard was looking forward to as an excuse for a gala event, not exactly what I wanted but if he wanted it . . . Anyway I shall have lunch here at the house in the Hollywood Hills with a producer and dinner with Doug Wick and Lucy Fisher as well as my nephew Burr Steers and his wife, Jennifer. Eighty sounds serious to me. Certainly when people ask "How are you feeling?" they are actually interested, for the moment at least, in your answer. Most people my age are safely dead and I must soon throw out my book of telephone numbers since nearly everyone in it has, as they used to say, fallen from the perch or ridden on ahead—mad euphemisms abound. But there are living voices on the telephone today, particularly from Europe where the birthdays of notables are noted. First call from Moscow: Tanya, one of my translators (aged eighty-four). She has a married daughter living in the Midwest and she will soon be visiting her. I say that I hope she won't be too distressed by the lunatic jingoism on every side. She is tactful. "I really only know you and Mailer and then I am in civilization." The voice trails off. Our roles are reversed; for thirty years she has apologized to me for Russian folly, now I . . . A fax from Germany. One from London. Soon the fax will characteristically break down. Meanwhile my face on the cover of Altman's book stares up at me from the partners desk which now accommodates a single solitary partner with few attachments. A friend recently diagnosed with lung cancer rings. I share what knowledge I have picked up during Howard's two-year siege. My Italian publisher Elido Fazi thinks that I should tell more about Howard but what does one say of a private relationship? This month there are three books about me: two by Australians, one by a Canadian. U.S. persons are not encouraged to contemplate the subject. Altman's is the most thorough study and deals with the numerous riptides, political and cultural, that I have encountered on my way to Rock Creek Cemetery.

Dennis Altman, author of *Gore Vidal's America*, is a professor of politics at La Trobe University in Melbourne, Australia. Much of this year he has been teaching at Harvard. I've known him slightly since 1973 when we appeared on the same TV program in Sydney. I value Altman's new book for his general reflections on sex, politics, and religion. But I was a bit jolted to read, early on, "Luckily there is no need here to do more than sketch briefly Vidal's life: it has been dealt with exhaustively in a biography by Fred Kaplan, which was written over a period of years during the 1990s and reflects, at times too much, Vidal's own perception of his life." Actually what it reflects is Kaplan's close reading of my first memoir, *Palimpsest*, which Altman seems to think I cobbled together *after* reading K.'s "exhaustive" biography. Altman also thinks I took my grandfather's name for my own "though he had been christened Eugene Luther Vidal." But I had been christened "Eugene Luther Gore Vidal" by the Reverend Albert Hawley Lucas, headmaster of St. Albans. When I started to publish stories I lopped off the first two names.

By and large Altman's errors are few and have to do only with me, his second lead after America. He does write that on enlisting in the army "[He] was too young for active service." But, of course, I was not too young. The army with characteristic bad faith had started an Army Specialized Training Program for high-school graduates. We were to be trained, among other things, in foreign languages to take our place in AMGOT the future Allied military government of the defeated Axis nations. So the army scooped up thousands of seventeen-year-olds and then when the Nazis began their counterattack in the so-called battle of the bulge the ASTPers were thrown, barely trained, into the infantry where many of my friends and classmates were killed. They were plainly not "too young for active service" but just right for "cannon fodder." Altman's most serious errors come when he writes that my "claim" that the daily *New York Times*, after *The City and the Pillar*, refused to review my next five novels is "inaccurate." He could have easily checked out the daily paper's list of books reviewed: it does not include *The Season of Comfort*; *A Search for the King*; *Dark Green, Bright Red*; *The Judgment of Paris*; *Messiah*; as well as, of course, the offending novel *The City and the Pillar*. A later editor of the Sunday *New York Times* weekly book review Rebecca Sinkler told me "you forgot a sixth book of yours that was ignored: *A Thirsty Evil*, the collection of your short stories."

Finally, Altman is always at his best when he does serious research. Just as the neocons found it necessary to smear Edward Said as a liar who had no real connection with Palestine, it also became necessary for them, in the light of my attack on Sharon for drawing the 1982 blood bath in Lebanon, to invent anti-Semitic quotes allegedly written by me. Altman thinks that this goes back to my "famous comment in 1959 that 'each year there is a short list of the OK writers. Today's list consists of two Jews, two Negroes, and a safe floating goy of the old American establishment just to show there is no prejudice in our loving land; only the poor old homosexualists are out.' " "The critic Leslie Fiedler acutely pointed out," writes Altman, "that 'the comment was written in mock horror but with an undertone of real bitterness too.' " Fiedler, a friend during the fifties when we were both living in Athens, is seldom acute in his efforts at criticism convinced as he was, at least back then, that

American WASP males were all homosexually inclined particularly in
the direction of the likes of Mark Twain's escaped slave Jim. My use of
the list was sardonic and was so perceived at the time. The "two Jews"
that I adverted to was to emphasize the point that the American literary
establishment had long been centered on the absolute primacy of
WASPs and so Jews were marginalized as writers and often proscribed
as teachers by college English Departments, to which the late Alfred
Kazin so often furiously testified; while African Americans were encouraged to go live in Paris as did Richard Wright and, in the end,
Jimmy Baldwin. His first book was turned down by E. P. Dutton where
I was then an associate editor and had tried for a year to get *Cry Holy*,
first title for *Go Tell It on the Mountain*, accepted by Dutton; but the
owner, Elliott Macrae, told me: "I can't publish Baldwin, I'm from Virginia." Altman thinks that I have largely ignored black literature. Politically minded African Americans are better informed. As recently as a
month ago Representative Cynthia McKinney invited me to address the
Black Caucus of the House of Representatives. I am also chided for not
doing enough about AIDS; but my virological skills are few.

FIFTY-TWO

———————— ✳ ————————

Once these fits of political correctness have passed, Altman has panned a nugget or two of purest gold in the great swamp that is Norman Podhoretz land. "The prominent neoconservative Norman Podhoretz, former editor of *Commentary*, has claimed that Vidal is clearly anti-Semitic: he identified a piece written by Vidal for the *Nation* in 1986 as 'the most blatantly and egregiously anti-Semitic outburst to have appeared in a respectable American periodical since World War II.' In the piece Podhoretz claims Vidal declared that 'the Jews were impoverishing the United States and bringing the world closer and closer to a nuclear war,' and warning that 'the Jews (never mind if they were born here or were naturalized citizens) had better watch out if they wished to stay on among us.'

"This would be damning," Altman concedes,

if indeed Vidal had written it. Checking the original article, to which Podhoretz himself referred me, I cannot find these alleged quotes.

What Vidal does say is: "He and Midge [his wife] stay on among us, in order to make propaganda and raise money for Israel—a country they don't seem eager to live in . . . Although there is nothing wrong with being a lobbyist for a foreign power, one is supposed to register with the Justice Department . . ."

Altman continues,

No mention of the warning to Jews. What is missed in those attacks on Vidal for anti-Semitism is any recognition of his sense of betrayal when some New York Jewish intellectuals, with whom he had mixed as a young writer, enthusiastically denounced the new gay movement. Midge Decter . . . at *Harper's Magazine* . . . published an article by Joseph Epstein in which he wrote: "If I had the power to do so I would wish homosexuality off the face of the earth." It was Vidal, not the Jewish Decter, who saw the striking parallel in this language to that used by Hitler.

Although the Bush administration has got us used to the telling of lies about such important matters as war and peace, the thriving cottage industry of ascribing to public figures words that they never said is less well known. But severe laws are in place with very severe penalties for those who, like Norman Podhoretz, simply invent inflammatory statements which he then ascribes to his numerous enemies as their actual words, a practice that should he persist in, he will be, under current law, prison-bound.

Altman occasionally has trouble keeping separate what my characters think and what I think: "Thus his historical novels refer often to Washington as an African city, without ever giving us a sense of how it might have seemed to the Africans." First, it is my character Caroline Sanford who was brought up in Europe who was startled to find Washington, D.C., "an African city." She expresses neither delight nor dismay at the fact she also becomes a friend of an "African" who is related to the black Jefferson family, a first family of the city. Altman then misreads my play *Weekend* in which the son of a presidential candidate marries an African American. Altman is upset by my jarringly superficial tone which, of course, is the whole point to the exercise: audiences in Washington, where the play first opened, were amused and relieved that the presidential candidate has no feeling at all about race nor does his wife; they only care about the coming election and will such a marriage as their son's be helpful. When they decide that it will be an electoral plus, there is a mock happy, even ecstatic, ending where they all remember to smile. Opportunism has won again. I am not a playwright who lectures audiences on good citizenship. I don't have to, as the Black Caucus might have enlightened Altman. He also makes strange leaps in the dark. He writes that the editors of *The New York Review of Books* "rejected some of Vidal's pieces particularly those seen as too strident in their criticism of Israel." There were no such pieces either written by me nor rejected by them. Our only political quarrels were over Robert Kennedy whose nimbus—bright to them—was not visible to me.

Altman is at his best when he meditates on Sex, Hollywood, Politics, and Religion. He has many wise things to say on those essential subjects which I have spent years trying to get into proper focus, particularly religion. Alongside Altman's book on my desk there are the uncorrected page proofs of a Duke University Press book called *How to Be an Intellectual in the Age of TV* subtitled "The Lessons of Gore Vidal," by Marcie Frank. I met Professor Frank during a panel discussion celebrating the fifty-fifth anniversary of the publication of *The City and the Pillar* at Yale's Davies Auditorium. Half a dozen writers/teachers read papers on that ancient novel to a crowd of several hundred interested parties, including myself. I recall Professor Frank's remarks as sharply witty and now they are the core of a book about how a public intellectual from the hot world of print can survive in the coolest medium of all, television. Frank recalled my idle remark some years ago: "Never

Here I am on *Laugh-In* in 1971 with June Gable, a marvelous comic who had invented a Latin huckster character called Esmeralda whose speech was surrealist. Here she is explaining to me how she is "an endangered feces."

pass up the opportunity to have sex or appear on television." Advice I would never give today in the age of AIDS and its television equivalent Fox News. Since *autre temps, autre moeurs* as Roseanne Barr might say. Frank links my remark to Andy Warhol's famous ecumenical prayer: "In the future, everyone will be famous for fifteen minutes." "Both," she writes,

> understand television as a transmissions apparatus that links the famous with their audience in a giant circle jerk . . . Many accounts of the public intellectual suggest that the species is virtually extinct, yet Vidal has been a veritable fixture on the American intellectual scene for the past forty years. Paradoxically, perhaps, his ubiquity in print, in politics, and on big and small screens has discouraged the recognition of his achievements, though a few have overcome the chronic resentment of celebrity that plagues those who tally such matters. For Edward Said, for instance, Vidal is an ideal example of the intellectual; however, this is because of his position as an independent (not institutionally affiliated) expatriate (Vidal moved to Italy in 1963, though in 2004 he returned to Los Angeles, where he has maintained a residence since 1978) . . . while he has been almost completely ignored by the academic literary establishment. Although recent interest, academic and other, in matters of gender and sexuality has prompted a slight increase in institutional attention to Vidal, his refusal to be labeled as gay and his insistence that no identities follow from sexual practices have proved problematic for those who would include him in a gay canon . . . Vidal has been slippery to categorize because he has consistently played against expectations. In blurring the fine line between insider and outsider, he redefined those boundaries . . . [H]e wrote *The City and the Pillar* (1948), the first American novel to depict homosexual sex explicitly, yet this did not stop him from running for public office twice, first for Congress in 1960, as a Democrat in heavily Republican upstate New York, and then for the Democratic nomination for Senate in 1982, against Jerry Brown.

Frank and others seem not to believe that by publishing *The City and the Pillar* I had permanently shut the door on a political career because I did run twice and in the first race got the most votes for a Democrat since 1910 and in the second got half a million votes while spending the least money in a field of nine candidates. But that was that. Hardly anyone goes into American politics without wanting to go, ultimately, all the way. But I could not, for demonstrable reasons. Although *The New York Times* never covered elections in the 29th Congressional District so far to the north of Times Square, they sent a special journalist called Ira Freeman to do the necessary ax job. He kept giggling nervously and repeating over and over again, "I don't know anything about politics." He did know how to smear, of course; and did.

Frank offers an account of the film *Visit to a Small Planet*, originally a play for television, then a play for Broadway and, finally, terminally, a movie with the dread Jerry Lewis who Frank tells us: "According to Lewis, it was Vidal's idea to cast him." It was Vidal's idea to cast David Niven and Paramount agreed; then Lewis, somehow, got the part which he played as a nine-year-old from outer space. Frank is a truly audacious explorer in the rain forest of my career. She finds shadowy monsters unknown to me and similarities where I find none. Jacqueline Susann was a popular novelist who exploited TV in her successful efforts to sell her exciting and excited novels, largely about feminine ailments and addictions. Although I have never read her I enjoyed meeting her several times with her large dark eyes whose thick false lashes resembled a pair of tarantulas in a postcoital state. Frank writes:

> But, like Susann, Jerry Lewis has much in common with Vidal's Myra. I put Vidal in the company of Susann (just as I put him in the company of Jerry Lewis earlier) in order to suggest an alternative genealogy for the intellectual, one excluded from those accounts that have been dominated by the print-based model of the intellectual.

If Vidal maintains the status of exemplary American writer-intellectual in the age of TV, it is because he has both exploited the print-screen circuit in the genre of romance and found ways to transmit his sexual politics on-screen.

Frank is very good on *Live from Golgotha* though its alleged subtitle is not "The Gospel According to Gore Vidal," an addition made by a creative dust-jacket designer. My Gospel would have been very different. "James Tatum has given a persuasive exposition of Vidal's adherence to the world of Roman which he calls Vidal's *Romanitas*. Underwriting Vidal's *Romanitas* is a universalism evident in his treatments of sexuality but also there in his mode of political address. The example of Vidal should thus prompt an alternative account of the intellectual and the media that would consider the prospects of universalism in our day." Now Ms. Frank is getting to the engine room of her subject. The first grown-up book that I read on my own was a nineteenth-century edition of *Tales from Livy* that I'd found in my grandfather's library. Although in school I was like so many others persecuted with Julius Caesar's *Gallic Wars* of which Montaigne observed that although every reader is eager to know why he was so brilliant a general, not to mention a transformer of the old republic into a principate suitable for himself, he tells us nothing interesting on those subjects so busy is he trying to convince us what a greater engineer he was. (I, though not a general, generalize like the emperor and god-to-be.) Frank handles this most originally:

Perversely, perhaps, when I call Vidal's intellectual career an *exercise in televisual classicism* I take my cue from the man whom Vidal obliterated from his alternative political history of the United States: Richard Nixon. It was Nixon who recognized and confirmed Vidal's classic status. When asked to what purposes he would put the auditorium of his presidential library, Nixon said that it should be used to reenact "great debates like—oh, Vidal and Buckley's 1968 battle" had brought sexuality into the political arena, something the non-charismatic, conservative Nixon would seem the least likely to have recognized, but here Nixon confers on Vidal and Buckley the status of national treasures.

FIFTY-THREE

---- ✳ ----

"Bemoaning the demise of the serious novel, or the disintegration of literary fame, as the consequence of the loss of history makes Vidal's satirical stance reminiscent of Alexander Pope. He thus might seem to support those who believe in the decline of the intellectual or of literary seriousness. But Vidal simultaneously overrides Pope's famous definition of wit—'What oft was thought but ne'er so well expressed'—by expressing it so well, so often, verbatim. Such reproduction, enabled by the central position of television in Vidal's writing, points to the future possibilities suggested by Myra's utopian mission, to 're-create the sexes and thus save the human race from certain extinction.' Exploiting the television commercial as 'the last demonstration of *necessary* love in the West,' Vidal successfully negotiates a public role for the author as intellectual on the basis of the circuit that he establishes between the page and the movie screen, a circuit that relies on the mediation of that amnesia-inducing and immortality-producing medium: the television. Vidal uses TV to ward off the blurring of the boundaries between culture and politics in identity-based politics. He exploits the congruencies among critiques of genetic, genital, and technological determinism. By these means, he has refused to be ghettoized . . . in TV he has found both a vehicle through which to convey his politics and a mode of address for a new televisual public, that is, a public conditioned by television even when it reads. Vidal's career teaches us that it is possible to remain a universal intellectual in the age of TV. He has done so by negotiating the print-screen circuit."

FIFTY-FOUR

———————— ✳ ————————

Irony has never had an easy time of it in our American version of English. We tend to bald bold literal statements whether it be during a sales pitch to someone who may be persuaded to buy a used car that once belonged to a blind octogenarian widow whose car had never accrued so much as a fraction of vulgar mileage. Lately I've noted that the notion of irony, if not irony itself, is suddenly abroad. Particularly on television. All sorts of young and not-so-young people when they say something that has a slightly tinny sound will, simultaneously, hold up both hands with forefingers extended on either side of the head to mean, I think, that the statement is in quotation marks because . . . well, what? That the statement for some reason is suspect? Untrue? Moot? Whatever the gesture means, I suspect that, at times, irony *may* be intended but the very concept of irony is unusual in our language featuring as it does enthusiastic declarative sentences sometimes true but if, in quotes, perhaps, false: so caveat auditor.

Since much of what I say and write tends to the ironic (without, however, the cute bracketing fingers) I should like to end this memoir with, first, a definition of irony and, second, a demonstration of irony in action that ended in catastrophic murder.

The best of dictionaries of English words and their usage is the *Oxford English Dictionary*. Here is their listing for "irony":

1) A figure of speech in which the intended meaning is the opposite of that expressed by the words used; usually taking the form of sarcasm or ridicule in which laudatory expressions are used to imply condemnation or contempt.

2) A condition of affairs or events of a character opposite to what was, or might naturally be, expected; a contradictory outcome of events as if in mockery of the promise and fitness of things.

Let's keep this last definition in mind as I now tell a tale for midnight.

In 1961 a new president of the United States, John F. Kennedy, was inaugurated at the age of forty-three. With him a new generation had taken the crown from the older generation as represented by General Eisenhower. There was triumphant talk of a new frontier presumably to be crossed by all of us into a new bright land where the only shadow that marred the prospect was that of the hideous, murderous specter of international Communism centered upon the Soviet Union against whom JFK had sworn to bear any burden to ensure the ultimate victory of freedom, liberty, and so on. But early on, starting in 1959, under the general direction of the then vice president Richard M. Nixon, who had many interesting Cuban Mob connections (yes, Bebe Rebozo his mysterious friend was also linked not only to mobsters but to the Cuban dictator Batista who had been overthrown by Fidel Castro to the annoyance of the Mob, an annoyance that turned to fury when Castro shut down, if only briefly, the Mafia-run Havana casinos). Elements of the CIA were soon attempting to murder Castro who, like all Nixon enemies, was if not yet a Communist, worse, a Communist dupe. The presidential election of 1960 was a close one fought by Nixon and John F. Kennedy, an attractive Massachusetts senator whose father had, ironically, dealings with many mobsters during the pre–World War Two period, as well as at the time of the prohibition of alcohol. The late film producer Ray Stark told me how, during the short presidency of JFK, Joe Kennedy and Frank Costello (the retired N.Y. Mob overlord) would often have dinner at Kennedy's Central Park South apartment and rehash old crimes, often in the company of a retired Teamster who gave great massages. Joe's Mob connections were useful to Jack in the 1960 election and could easily have saved JFK's life in 1963 had Bobby Kennedy, in the interest of building himself up in the public's eyes, not started arresting important mobsters particularly in the so-called Apalachin Mob Conference bust where they had all come together to confer about the succession to the leadership of the New York Mob. I've long since forgotten how I first heard of the plot to kill JFK, while I had no idea at all of the Kennedy brothers' plot to kill Castro on December 1, 1963, until I read a recent book by Lamar Waldron and Thom Hartmann called *Ultimate Sacrifice*. It was assumed that the Cuban Missile Crisis of 1962 had sufficiently alarmed JFK and Castro's mentor, Khrushchev, so that they jointly backed down, putting an end, so everyone thought, to such dangerous adventures. JFK had pledged not to invade Cuba *if* Castro would allow inspections of any remaining missiles on the island. Since Castro did not cooperate, JFK then regarded his pledge as inoperative. "In the spring of 1963," according to *Ultimate Sacrifice* (more a literal than an ironic title), "John and Robert Kennedy started laying the groundwork for a coup against Fidel Castro that would eventually be set for what they called C-Day: December, 1 1963." Bobby, like Nixon before him, was in charge of what would be the most secretive operation of its sort in our history. Since the CIA had, in the eyes of the Kennedys, botched the 1961 Bay of Pigs invasion, the Department of Defense was to be in charge of this adventure which would first engage Mob hit men to assassinate Castro and then replace him with a provisional government that would implore the United States to come to its aid and restore order. Ours is a society riddled with plots of every kind from, let's say, one to bribe certain members of Congress to cheat the Indians of their casino money to the financing, often secretly, of numerous presidential elections while, simultaneously, great companies like Enron cheat customers, stockholders, employees; yet anyone who draws attention to all of this corruption is quickly denounced as a conspiracy theorist who means to undo the great fiction that anything truly wicked, at least in the murder line, must be the work of a sole solitary "nut" who is simply Evil; hence, the setting up of Lee Harvey Oswald as the lone crazed killer of JFK despite his own brief but presumably accurate statement after his Dallas arrest: "I'm the patsy"; then, as planned, his being gunned down by Jack Ruby, a fellow CIA "asset" (I use dumb quotes denoting that neither, strictly speaking, was a *real* asset in the literal sense but each had a role to play); Oswald as lone killer for no reason at all and addled Ruby, a onetime Chicago mobster, who claimed to be deeply worried about the stress that all this must be causing the widow Kennedy.

FIFTY-FIVE

———— ✳ ————

I shall now borrow *Publishers Weekly*'s nice précis of this long highly detailed book, which states that Gerald Posner's polemic, *Case Closed* (1993),

> took the CIA's lack of involvement for granted, and that, according to this mammoth and painstakingly researched account, was a big mistake. It is Waldron and Hartmann's . . . contention—bolstered by access to many previously unavailable files, and interviews with little-known as well as prominent figures—that the CIA knew a great deal about the assassination. But the agency couldn't admit what it knew because that could uncover the existence of a U.S. plan for a coup in Cuba, run by JFK's brother, Attorney General Robert Kennedy. The assassination, say the authors, was carried out by hired gunmen on the orders of three noted Mafia dons whose lives were being made miserable by RFK's ruthless pursuit—and these Mafia men knew about the planned invasion because they had worked with the CIA on previous efforts to topple Castro. Oswald,

long a hidden CIA agent, was set up as the patsy, and it had always been Jack Ruby's job to eliminate him if he wasn't killed at the scene of Kennedy's shooting. How do the authors make their case? With a relentless accumulation of detail, a very thorough knowledge of every political and forensic detail and the broad perspective of historians rather than assassination theorists.

Ultimate Sacrifice describes how the Kennedy C-Day plan was penetrated by three Mafia godfathers—Carlos Marcello (New Orleans), Santo Trafficante (Tampa, Florida), and Johnny Roselli (out of Chicago). All three were being vigorously pursued by Attorney General Robert Kennedy, along with a dozen of their associates of whom six were also working on the Castro murder case. The crime bosses then used parts of the C Plan, aka AMWorld, to arrange JFK's assassination in a way that would prevent a thorough government investigation in order to protect the Coup Plan, its participants, as well as, naturally, national security by invoking the secrecy surrounding the C Plan. The Mob bosses targeted JFK twice before Dallas, once in Chicago on November 2 (JFK called off his motorcade) and then in Tampa on November 18 (he survived unscathed). *Ultimate Sacrifice* reveals and details why Robert Kennedy later told several close associates the name of the godfather (Carlos Marcello) who had ordered his brother killed—but he couldn't do anything about it for fear the Soviets might go to war: Irony in tragic action . . . I recall when over the years I'd be asked why what happened at Dallas happened, I'd answer: "Because Bobby had broken a truce made with the Mob by Joe Kennedy in 1960. Bobby, seeking glory, broke it by hounding Teamster boss Hoffa, and going after the Mob bosses": in the case of Carlos Marcello of New Orleans (and sometimes Havana), Bobby had him deported to Guatemala. Trafficante, a Florida boss, was recorded as telling Marcello that they must kill Bobby but Marcello said no. "When a dog bothers you, you don't cut off its tail." Thus was the murder of JFK ordered and carried out by the same team that his brother was assembling to murder Castro and prepare the way for an invasion of Cuba at the request of a Kennedy-selected provisional government. This is classic irony and on the bloodiest scale. Had word leaked out, the Soviets in order to avenge Castro might have used its nuclear-tipped missiles against some fifty U.S. cities. Hence, the use of Oswald as patsy and his murder by a fellow CIA agent Jack Ruby: the transcript of Ruby's later quizzing by a clueless Chief Justice Earl Warren is worthy of that non-ironist Samuel Beckett.

FIFTY-SIX

————— ✳ —————

Professor Marcie Frank has flattered me by a comparison to Pope. So, in ending, let me quote the last lines of the *Dunciad*, lines that I learned, voluntarily, as a schoolboy:

> *Nor public flame nor private, dares to shine;*
> *Nor human spark is left, nor glimpse divine!*
> *Lo! thy dread empire, CHAOS! is restor'd;*
> *Light dies before thy uncreating word;*
> *Thy hand, great Anarch, lets the curtain fall,*
> *And universal Darkness buries all.*

In 1943 when I recited this to a classmate at the Phillips Exeter Academy, he was bewildered. "Why did you learn that?" he asked. "Because," I said, "it's bound to be apt one of these days." And so it is today, January 1, 2006.

Much time over thirty years was spent on the balcony overlooking the Tyrrhenian Sea. Ulysses, more than usually off course, was believed to have sailed . . . well, rowed on the scenic route back home to Ithaca. Several miles to the back of my head are the temples of Paestum.

PHOTO CREDITS

————— ✳ —————

Photography research by Ann Schneider

INDEX

———— ✳ ————

Page numbers in *italics* refer to illustrations.

ABOUT THE AUTHOR

——————— ✳ ———————

Gore Vidal is the author of twenty-five novels, six plays, many screenplays, more than two hundred essays, and the critically lauded memoir *Palimpsest*. Vidal's *United States: Essays 1952–1992* won the 1993 National Book Award.

PALIMPSEST

Gore Vidal

'Wonderfully entertaining. You want high-level political gossip?
You get it here. There is no one who was anyone whom he has
not met, and although some receive magisterial putdowns, he is
generous to more, including old rivals like Mailer . . . [readers]
will be richly rewarded, for it offers all the zing of a Dry Martini
without the danger of getting drunk'
Daily Telegraph

'He does not narrate his life: he reviews it. He quotes from diaries,
letters and books, even enlisting the support of his own essays
and fiction. The result is something quite novel and wonderfully
appealing, a critical biography of himself . . . [with] an enchanting
set of stories about household names – Vidal's life
might even be his greatest work'
Independent

'I thought I was wise to all his moves, I knew Vidal would
have me frowning and nodding and smiling and smirking – with
admiration, with exasperation, with scandalised dissent. I never
dreamed Vidal would have me wiping my eyes, and staring wanly
out of the window, and emitting strange sighs . . . Approaching
seventy, Vidal now takes cognisance of the human heart,
and reveals that he has one'
Sunday Times

Abacus
978-0-349-10800-1

Now you can order superb titles directly from Abacus

☐	Palimpsest	Gore Vidal	£10.99
☐	United States	Gore Vidal	£15.99
☐	Washington DC	Gore Vidal	£9.99
☐	Myra Breckinridge	Gore Vidal	£9.99

The prices shown above are correct at time of going to press. However, the publishers reserve the right to increase prices on covers from those previously advertised, without further notice.

───────────────── ⬭ ABACUS ⬭ ─────────────────

Please allow for postage and packing: **Free UK delivery.**
Europe: add 25% of retail price; Rest of World: 45% of retail price.

To order any of the above or any other Abacus titles, please call our credit card orderline or fill in this coupon and send/fax it to:

Abacus, PO Box 121, Kettering, Northants NN14 4ZQ
Fax: 01832 733076   Tel: 01832 737527
Email: aspenhouse@FSBDial.co.uk

☐ I enclose a UK bank cheque made payable to Abacus for £ . . . .
☐ Please charge £ . . . . . . to my Visa/Delta/Maestro

Expiry Date ☐☐☐☐   Maestro Issue No. ☐☐

NAME (BLOCK LETTERS please) . . . .

ADDRESS . . . .

. . . .

. . . .

Postcode . . . . Telephone . . . .

Signature . . . .

Please allow 28 days for delivery within the UK. Offer subject to price and availability.

Please do not send any further mailings from companies carefully selected by Abacus ☐